Stalingrad 1942–43

COMBAT

German Soldier

VERSUS

Soviet Soldier

Chris McNab

Osprey Publishing
c/o Bloomsbury Publishing Plc
PO Box 883, Oxford, OX1 9PL, UK
Or
c/o Bloomsbury Publishing Inc.
1385 Broadway, 5th Floor, New York, NY 10018, USA
E-mail: info@ospreypublishing.com

www.ospreypublishing.com

OSPREY is a trademark of Osprey Publishing Ltd, a division of
Bloomsbury Publishing Plc.

First published in Great Britain in 2017

© 2017 Osprey Publishing Ltd

ISBN: PB: 978 1 4728 2456 1
        ePub: 978 1 4728 2457 8
        ePDF: 978 1 4728 2458 5
        XML: 978 1 4728 2459 2

17 18 19 20 21   10 9 8 7 6 5 4 3 2 1

Index by Rob Munro
Typeset in Univers, Sabon and Adobe Garamond Pro
Cartography by bounford.com
Page layouts by PDQ Digital Media Solutions, Bungay, UK
Printed in China through World Print Ltd.

Osprey Publishing supports the Woodland Trust, the UK's leading
woodland conservation charity. Between 2014 and 2018 our donations
are being spent on their Centenary Woods project in the UK.

To find out more about our authors and books visit **www.
ospreypublishing.com**. Here you will find extracts, author interviews,
details of forthcoming events and the option to sign up for our newsletter.

Acknowledgements

I would like to thank Jason D. Mark for his kind permission to
reproduce several extensive passages of his Stalingrad research.
Thanks also go to bounford.com for their preparation of the involved
cartography for this title, and to Nick Reynolds, commissioning editor at
Osprey Publishing, for his unfailing guidance in presenting some of the
complexities of the Stalingrad battle.

Editor's note

In this book measurements are given in metric units of measurement.
The following data will help when converting between imperial and
metric measurements:

1km = 0.62 miles
1m = 1.09yd
1m = 3.28ft
1m = 39.37in
1cm = 0.39in
1mm = 0.04in
1kg = 2.20lb

Key to military symbols

Key to unit identification

CONTENTS

Introduction

It can appear rather sensationalist to rank battles according to the ever-popular 'worst in history' scale. Typically, the rankings are based on casualty counts and the sheer number of participants, human and (if relevant) mechanical. Using such a blunt metric ignores the fact that the *intensity* of action is not so easily measured, if we push the consideration down to the human level. A small-unit action, for example, might last just three or four hours and produce only a few dozen casualties, but the brutality of the localized fighting during those hours could be extreme. Any armchair judgement about warfare must always be made from a position of humility, after all, and ranking battles purely according to sheer size runs the risk of treating individual participants as so much statistical data.

This being said, the battle of Stalingrad does have a justified claim to at least some privileged study in the history of warfare. Fought between August 1942 and early February 1943, the battle was indeed conducted on an apocalyptic scale, with an approximate casualty count of nearly two million men dead, wounded or captured. This statistic alone makes Stalingrad possibly the most costly clash in history, in terms of human attrition. It also ticks the box for strategic significance. The first great army-level defeat for German forces in World War II, Stalingrad marked the turning point in Hitler's fortunes; from February 1943 onwards, the overall trajectory of the Wehrmacht was retreat back to the homeland and eventual defeat.

So, on the counts of both scale and impact, Stalingrad looms large over military history; and yet, these factors do not entirely account for the sombre fascination with this clash on the Volga River. The terrible, defining element of Stalingrad was the unrelenting brutality of the fighting. Although the city was destroyed by heavy weaponry, it was the submachine gun (SMG), sniping rifle, pistol, grenade, demolition charge, dagger and sharpened spade that frequently decided the fight within the city limits, backed by supporting armour and artillery. During World War II, opposing armies often faced each

A Soviet infantryman moves cautiously through the Stalingrad rubble, his 7.62mm PPSh-41 SMG at the ready. Note how a sagging floor structure provides the soldier with overhead cover; such obscuration was essential for any soldier in Stalingrad looking to avoid enemy snipers or fire from upper floors. (AirSeaLand Photos/ Cody Images)

other with little more than a few hundred metres between their respective front lines. At Stalingrad, no man's land essentially did not exist, the distance between the opposing forces being measured in courtyards, corridors, walls and factory floors. The effect of this proximity was powerfully captured by one German officer of 24. Panzer-Division:

> We have fought for fifteen days for a single house with mortars, grenades, machine guns and bayonets. Already by the third day fifty-four German corpses are strewn in the cellars, on the landings, and the staircases. The front is a corridor between burnt-out rooms; it is the thin ceiling between two floors. Help comes from neighbouring houses by fire escapes and chimneys. There is a ceaseless struggle from noon to night. From storey to storey, faces black with sweat, we bombed each other with grenades in the middle of explosions, clouds of dust and smoke ... Ask any soldier what hand-to-hand struggle means in such a fight. And imagine Stalingrad; eighty days and eighty nights of hand-to-hand struggle. (Anon)

It is in this context, of the close-quarters warfare, that we sharpen our focus on two of the Stalingrad combatants – the German combat engineer and the Red Army rifleman; a story of the clash between highly trained specialists and battle-hardened generalists. The German combat engineers, collectively known as *Pioniere* (pioneers), were a skilled fusion of assault troops and field technicians, organized in battalion-sized units within German infantry and Panzer divisions. Injected more deliberately into the battle of Stalingrad in November 1942, the *Pioniere* were seen as a fresh tip on the spear, one that could hopefully alter the balance in the close-quarters fighting in Stalingrad against a frustratingly dogged Soviet defence.

The training and capabilities of the combat engineers was both practically broad and militarily useful. They aided the flow of logistics under combat conditions by laying tracks, constructing improvised bridges and pontoons across rivers, and assisting water crossings with assault boats or inflatable craft. They would lay or build all manner of defensive arrangements – minefields, booby traps, tank obstacles, infantry bunkers, camouflaged supply routes, machine-gun and mortar emplacements. On the attack, the *Pioniertruppen* were also specialists in destroying enemy fortifications and defensive positions using flamethrowers, grenades, smoke and explosive charges, working in conjunction

Explained in broad brushstrokes, Operation *Blue* was Hitler's attempt both to force the Soviet forces to their knees in a final cataclysmic defeat (Hitler constantly predicted that the Red Army was close to collapse), while also solving Germany's oil-supply problems by capturing the oilfields of the Caucasus. The initial plan was for Heeresgruppe Süd to strike out from its front line east of Kursk and Kharkov, with 2. Armee, 4. Panzerarmee, 6. Armee, Hungarian Second Army, Italian Eighth Army plus XXIX. Armeekorps (together grouped as Heeresgruppe B in July 1942) pushing down the Donets Corridor towards Stalingrad. They would secure the northern flank of the operation on the Don River, while 1. Panzerarmee and 17. Armee (from July, Heeresgruppe A, which included 11. Armee and Romanian Third Army) drove down to the south against the Caucasian oilfields.

Note that at this stage of planning, the oilfields were the primary objective, not the city of Stalingrad. This situation would change, however, as Hitler impatiently began modifying his plan following its launch on 28 June. The extent of the territory Heeresgruppe A would have to occupy was enlarged, to reach far down the shores of the Caspian Sea. For Heeresgruppe B, the city of Stalingrad now became an actual objective, a distant – and, many would argue, unnecessary – focus. Furthermore, Heeresgruppe B's ability to achieve this objective was hampered by Hitler's interference with the role of 4. Panzerarmee. On 17 July, Hitler diverted this force to support Heeresgruppe A in its push out of the Donets Basin across the Don around Rostov; it would continue the momentum of this drive deep into the Caucasus throughout the summer and into the winter of 1942. Thus 6. Armee, under its new commander General der Panzertruppe Friedrich von Paulus, with its Hungarian and Italian support, pushed on alone against tough opposition, crossing the Don elbow and reaching the Volga to the north of Stalingrad by 23 August.

During those summer months, despite Hitler's interference, the two German army groups made good progress, pushing five Soviet fronts (the equivalent of a German army group) back in the process. On the Soviet side, Stalin reacted with his predictable combination of panic and ruthlessness as his bridgeheads on the Don progressively collapsed by mid-August. Stalingrad, the very name of which denotes Stalin's special psychological connection to the city, was to be protected by its own front, the Stalingrad Front, created on 12 July. On 28 July, he issued an infamous order (No. 227) commanding that at Stalingrad Soviet forces would take 'Not one step back!' In short, the Red Army would fight to the death for the city. As the German forces edged ever closer to Stalingrad, the Soviet military and civilian forces were mobilized in a massive effort to fortify the city, digging endless kilometres of anti-tank trenches and creating chains of defensive positions.

Back on the German side, the fortunes of Heeresgruppe B appeared to have improved on 31 July, when Hitler once again vacillated, and reassigned 4. Panzerarmee back to the drive on Stalingrad. On 17 August, Paulus's 6. Armee crossed the Don and was advancing strongly on the Volga, forcing several Soviet armies back towards Stalingrad. German forces reached the Volga on 23 August, the same day on which Luftflotte 4 unleashed a devastating bombing raid on the city, killing tens of thousands of civilians yet ironically making the city more defensively obstinate, by increasing the complexity of the terrain. Now Hitler made another fatal mistake. Instead of opting for isolating or bypassing Stalingrad, he sent his forces into the heart of the city to fight it out street by street. The core element of the Stalingrad defence would be the 62nd Army, commanded by Lieutenant-General Vasily Ivanovich Chuikov. To the south was the 64th Army, under Lieutenant-General Mikhail Stepanovich Shumilov.

By November 1942, the battle of Stalingrad already looked very different from anything that Hitler had conceived of earlier in the year. It had evolved, rather against original intentions, to become the focal point of Operation *Blue*, the ambitious offensive launched back in June 1942, rather than a sideshow – a fact that would spell disaster for the German 6. Armee and for Hitler's war plans generally.

To understand the battles that followed, we need a sense of Stalingrad's layout. Stalingrad ran on a south-west axis, a slender city about 18km long and mostly hugging the western bank of the Volga. The northern part of the city was the Factory District, so called on account of its domination by several major industrial plants. This district was in itself divided into three sectors, from north to south: the Tractor Factory sector, focused upon the Dzerzhinsky Tractor Factory; the Barricades sector (Barrikady Gun Factory); and the Red October sector (Krasnyi Oktyabr/Red October Factory). Immediately south of Red October was the Mamaev Kurgan sector, named after the dominant height there. The Mamaev Kurgan itself was transformed into a heavily defended position by the Soviets, and for a time Chuikov had his headquarters there, although it was captured and lost several times by the Germans. South of the Mamaev Kurgan was basically the city centre, which alongside shops and houses included some important features, such as the Central Station and a major grain silo.

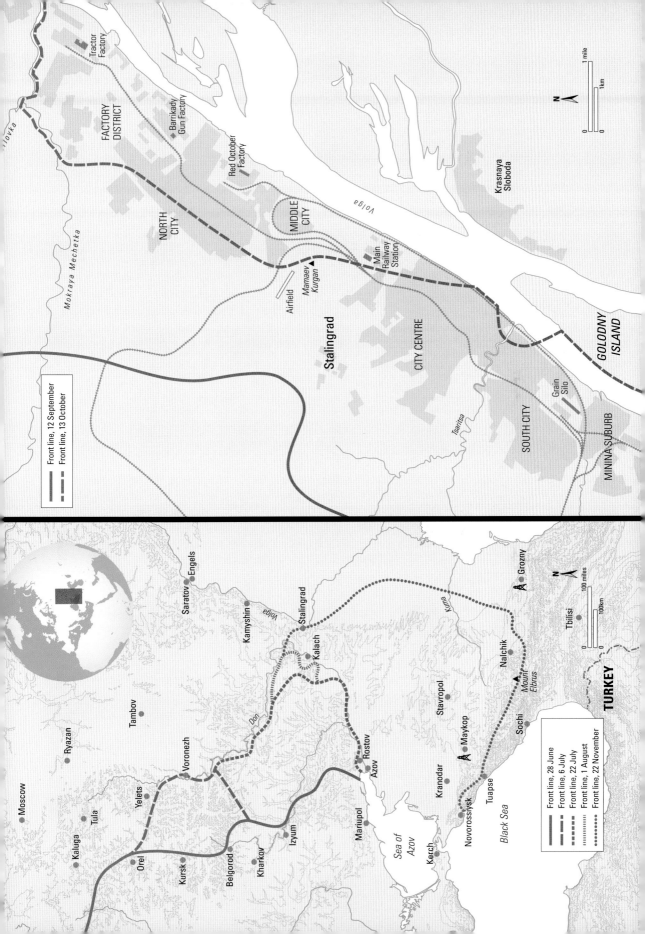

with German armour and infantry. They were also adept at blowing up virtually anything, from bridges and railway lines to factory buildings and machinery. As author Gordon Rottman states, the combat engineers 'were thought of as assault troops first and construction workers second' (Rottman 2010: 4).

The Soviet rifleman was, by contrast, the product of highly variable training, but also – if he survived – intense and quickly acquired combat experience, fused with the fierce motivation to fight that came from political threat (the noose and gun of the NKVD were ever present) and the willpower derived from defending home territory. By the time of the battle of Stalingrad, the Soviets had absorbed losses on a scale that would have defeated most other nations. Yet with resilience, the Red Army reformed itself, and hard-won experience and new command relations led to a sharpened tactical understanding, such as the development of offensive 'storm units' in urban warfare, better comprehension of how to create interlocked defensive positions, and a new competency in anti-tank warfare.

As we shall see in the clashes between these two forces, several popular and prevalent myths about the battle of Stalingrad are broken. The first is that the German forces were not suited to urban combat, but rather to the open manoeuvre warfare of *Blitzkrieg* operations. This is simply not true. Not only the combat engineer, but also the regular German infantryman, proved himself a first-rate practitioner of urban fighting. What can be said is that the German forces were vulnerable to the attrition of urban fighting, and that city fighting was often not the best application of their tactical focus, but such is not to say that they were not formidable opponents within the fabric of a town or city. The second myth is that the Soviet infantryman was scarcely trained cannon fodder, accomplishing through sheer manpower what he couldn't achieve through skill at arms. This is also untrue. Through the aforementioned experiences, among both soldiers and officers, and a steady improvement in tactics and some aspects of training, the Red Army soldier himself became a skilled practitioner of close-quarters fighting. Indeed, it seems to have been a type of warfare at which the Soviets excelled. Given the martial prowess of the two sides, it was inevitable that the three actions studied here were brutal and unforgiving.

This striking photograph shows a German assault force readying itself for an attack, heavily laden with small arms and grenades. An MG 34 machine gun (held by the man roughly in the centre of the group) has been fitted with a 50-round *Gurttrommel* drum magazine, which could be more convenient in assault manoeuvres than a loose belt. (Photo by Universal History Archive/UIG via Getty Images)

The Opposing Sides

PERSONAL WEAPONS

The tools of war used by the German combat engineers and their Soviet infantry opponents were in many ways similar. Being front-line assault troops, the emphasis was naturally upon small arms, grenades and portable demolition charges. As we shall see, however, the *Pioniertruppen* did have access to more specialist combat equipment, though the availability of such equipment was naturally constrained once the Soviets had encircled Stalingrad following their massive counter-offensive operation, Operation *Gallop*, launched on 13 January 1943. It is worth studying the small arms and individual weaponry of both sides at some length, as they had such a fundamental influence within the ruins of the city.

For both sides in the battle of Stalingrad, the key infantry weapons were the pistol, rifle, SMG, machine gun and grenade – the personal small arms upon which the soldiers' lives so often depended. The qualitative and sometimes quantitative differences between Soviet and German small arms, however, do make this a topic of significance to the battle itself.

German

In terms of personal firepower, German combat engineers were largely armed much as the rest of the German Army. The standard rifle was the 7.92mm Mauser Kar 98k, a shortened evolution of the original Mauser M1898. Although bolt-action rifles scarcely seem the most compelling weapons in a military arsenal, the Kar 98k offered important attributes to the German soldier. It was utterly reliable, thanks to the proven Mauser action, so the soldier could rely on it continuing to work even in the most extreme conditions. (It still required careful field maintenance, of course, as ice build-up during the winter months could lock the bolt solid if not cleared.)

German infantry study the terrain carefully in the factories of Stalingrad. Note how the man on the left has obscured the sharp profile and the shiny metal of his helmet with a cloth; numerous German soldiers died from sniper head shots after inadvertently exposing their heads for just a few seconds. Beyond rifles, SMGs and machine guns, some combat engineers would also carry pistols. Such weapons mainly sat in holsters on the hips of officers, but other soldiers would attempt to acquire them, as they proved very useful portable back-up fire for last-ditch actions, of which there were many in Stalingrad. Having a pistol also meant a combat engineer could use his hands to perform engineering duties, but still have a weapon on which to draw if needed. The classic German pistol models were three varieties of 9mm recoil-operated handgun – the Parabellum P08, the Walther P38 and the less-well-known Steyr M1912 – plus the redoubtable 7.63mm Mauser M1932 'Broomhandle' pistol might make an appearance. (AirSeaLand Photos/Cody Images)

It fired the powerful 7.92×57mm Mauser M98 round, which had excellent penetration and a killing range of more than 1km. The rifle was also accurate up to 600m, and, with the right sights, could exceed this.

Yet as good as the Kar 98k was, it had some profound limitations in a close-quarters arena such as Stalingrad, as did all bolt-action rifles. It had a limited internal ammunition box – just five rounds – which meant that constant reloading was required in intense firefights. The weapon being bolt-action, each round had to be manually chambered by the operation of the bolt. This specific action only took about a second, but factor in the time spent getting the rifle back on target, and operating the bolt could provide a lethal window of opportunity for an enemy to bring his weapon to bear. The range of the rifle was useful in open field conditions, but in close-quarters action this was scarcely relevant.

For these reasons, SMGs were popular alternatives to rifles in Stalingrad. Within a German pioneer section, which in combat tended to be about 8–10 men, the 9mm MP 40 (the standard SMG by late 1942) was typically held just by the section leader, an NCO. Yet for the other men in the actual fighting conditions of Stalingrad, acquiring an SMG either from resupply or simply by taking the weapon of a dead man made sense, as the SMG type fitted perfectly with the tactical realities of close-quarters combat. The MP 40 was a decent enough SMG, firing at a rate of 500rd/min. Its one key deficiency was the single-stack 32-round box magazine, which was not only prone to misfeeding rounds and being damaged, but also very long, making prone firing a challenge to torso and shoulders. In Stalingrad, soldiers would often switch from their rifles to an SMG if one became available, the SMG offering the advantages of full-automatic fire, a large magazine capacity, and no need for manual reloading, such advantages proving to be critical in urban warfare.

For heavier support fire, combat-engineer battalions could rely on around a dozen light machine guns (LMGs) plus any similar weapons mounted upon supporting vehicles such as motorcycles and sidecars or half-tracks. The standard German LMG, or rather the *Einheitsmaschinengewehr* (Universal Machine Gun, or what we would call the general-purpose machine gun), was the 7.92mm MG 34. In October 1942, the 7.92mm MG 42 also appeared in the German armed forces. Chief differences between the two were that the MG 34 was more expensive to produce, needed more careful battlefield maintenance and provided a slower rate of fire than the cheaper MG 42 (800rd/min as opposed to the MG 42's blistering 1,200rd/min). Note, however, that the MG 42 seems to have been a relative rarity in Stalingrad, although a handful of photographs do appear to show the newer weapon in service there.

A central area of expertise within the German *Pioniertruppen* was demolitions, a skill that was uniquely applicable to the fighting in Stalingrad. All German troops, including combat engineers, relied upon hand grenades for close-quarters explosive effects. In addition to grenades, the pioneers had

An MG 34 team waits to make its next move. In standard infantry and combat-engineer distribution, each section of roughly ten men (the exact numbers were in a state of flux in late 1942, especially in Stalingrad) would typically have an MG 34 or (later) an MG 42 team to provide fire support, this team consisting of a gunner, a loader (who also carried spare barrels) and an ammunition carrier. The MG 34 was an excellent weapon – belt-fed, fast-firing, largely reliable, portable, and with devastating effects on target – but the real advantage it offered was that it could be configured to different purposes via its mounts. Set on a tripod, for example, it could put down sustained support or defensive fire from a fixed position; fired from its integral bipod, in contrast, it could be kept mobile with the assault teams, giving them a ready supply of heavy firepower when needed. (AirSeaLand Photos/Cody Images)

3kg

This plate shows an *Obergefreiter* (an NCO rank) in Pionier-Bataillon 162, one of the combat-engineer units at the vanguard of the 11 November assault around the Barrikady Gun Factory. The soldier is already a veteran of the Eastern Front, his battalion having been involved in the Soviet campaign since June 1941. The advance to Stalingrad has weathered the soldiers physically from the distances travelled and the labour conducted under the scorching Russian summer, and psychologically from the experiences of combat during the battles on the approaches to the Don and Stalingrad in August and September. Nevertheless, the battalion had spent several weeks resting in rear areas before the 11 November offensive.

Weapons, dress and equipment

This soldier carries an MP 40 SMG (**1**) and also a 3kg *Geballteladungen* demolition charge (**2**), the latter useful for blowing holes in walls and for demolishing other obstacles. His uniform is that worn by most German infantry on the Eastern Front (and indeed elsewhere) during this year and season. He is wearing the field-grey M40 tunic (**3**), with its four large pockets, and matching trousers, and his rank is indicated by the sleeve stripes (**4**). Branch of service is shown via the black edging of the buttoned-down shoulder straps (**5**). The trousers are tucked into a set of brown canvas *Gamaschen* (gaiters; **6**), which would go some way to keeping out the ingress of dust, dirt and (later) snow into his boots. In terms of the boots themselves, this soldier is not wearing the classic German jackboot, but instead has *Schnurschuhe* combat ankle boots (**7**), much preferred by the German combat engineers. He is also kitted out in the M1940

Stahlhelm (steel helmet; **8**), which would provide basic protection from shell splinters or the glancing blow from a bullet, but little resistance to a full-power rifle or machine-gun bullet hitting square on at close–medium range of a few hundred metres.

As he is shown in the midst of an assault, he is wearing pure combat gear. One distinctive item is the *Pioniersturmgepäck* (Pioneer Assault Pack; **9**), a special type of load-carrying equipment used for engineer operations; about one-fifth of the battalion combat soldiers would wear one. It was composed of a backpack and side packs, and designed to hold multiple demolition charges, smoke pots and grenades. The right-side pouch had a rubber lining and was intended for a gas mask (although often repurposed), and the multiple small pockets were for five-round rifle clips. Sticking out of the pack are the handles of Stielhandgranate 24 stick grenades (**10**).

The soldier at the rear of this fire team is carrying a Stielhandgranate 24 (StG 24) – the famous German 'stick' grenade – attached to his pack for easy access. The standard-issue models were the StG 24 or newer StG 39 variant, and the less-well-known Einhandgranate 39, an 'egg'-type fragmentation grenade. Multiple stick-grenade heads could be tied around a central grenade head with wire, to boost the explosive effect on target. The stick of the German grenades provided extra throwing leverage compared to 'egg'-type grenades, meaning that a soldier with a strong throwing arm could hurl one out to about 35m. (AirSeaLand Photos/Cody Images)

access to a broad and occasionally specialist range of explosives for demolition and assault tasks. Demolition charges were available in a variety of weights and formats: a 100g boring cartridge (Bohrpatrone 28); 200g demolition container (Sprengkörper 28); 1kg demolition petard (Sprengbüsche 24); 3kg and 10kg concentrated charges (Geballteladungen), fitted in handled containers for ease of portability; and 3kg ball charge (Kugelladung 3kg), essentially like a massive egg grenade, used for pushing through emplacement embrasures. For the penetration of armour plate and other reinforced structures, the pioneers could rely on hefty monsters such as the 12.5kg shaped charge (Hohlladung 12.5kg), capable of punching through 76mm of armour, or for truly obdurate defences, the two-section 50kg hollow-charge device, which could penetrate up to 250mm of armour. (Such hardened targets were a relative rarity in Stalingrad, but heavy shaped-charge demolitions were still useful for destroying bunkers massively reinforced with rubble, sandbags and logs.) There was also the Hafthohlladung-Granate 3kg, a shaped charge fitted to a base consisting of three magnets, which enabled the soldier to clamp the mine to the outside of an armoured vehicle, ignite the 7-second fuse, and retreat to a safe distance before detonation. Note that this weapon could also be fitted with a 4-second fuse, for use when it was going to be thrown, although given the weight of the device the distance it could be hurled was not great.

Other pyrotechnics were also practical battlefield tools for the combat engineers. For generating smoke – a key element in masking an attack – the soldiers had either standard smoke grenades, of both egg and stick varieties, or larger devices that could deliver smoke over a wider area and for a longer duration. The two principal types were the small Rauchrohr Nebel 1939 smoke candle, 25mm in diameter and 250mm long with a 3–4-minute burn duration, and the larger Nebelkerzen 39 2.2kg can device that threw out a dense cloud of smoke for 4–7 minutes. For cutting barbed-wire defences, but also doubling up for various other assault purposes, there was the Rohrladung, Stahl, 3kg (3kg tube charge), essentially the German equivalent of the Allied 'Bangalore torpedo'.

At the beginning of the war, a *Pionier-Bataillon* was meant to have within its resources 351kg of explosive charges, 2,600m of detonating cord, 936 smoke candles and grenades plus more than 3,000 anti-personnel or anti-tank mines. This lavish allocation of resources was, by the time of Stalingrad, rather fanciful, and the levels of equipment available became ever more restricted as the German supply lines stretched ever further across southern Russia and the Ukraine. As such, some of the heavier and more specialist devices, such as the 50kg hollow charge or the Hafthohlladung-Granate 3kg, became relative rarities. Still, the combat engineers made good use of what they had. Note that as well as the standard German Army uniform and load-bearing equipment the combat engineers used, roughly one in five men also had a specialist three-compartment assault pack. The large central backpack was specifically designed to hold a combination of smoke grenades and demolition charges (two smoke grenades and a 3kg charge was a recommended load), while the

A German flamethrower operator puts down a short burst onto a Russian building from his Flammenwerfer 35. There is no doubt that the flamethrower had a definite utility in Stalingrad. A half-second burst against the window of a defended house might be all that was needed to suppress the position, either through inflicting flame injuries or, more commonly, through inducing suffocation by consuming the proximate air. Yet flamethrower operators were vulnerable. Contrary to Hollywood depictions, flamethrowers are not generally likely to explode, at least if hit by standard ball rounds, although hits by tracer or cannon rounds on the fuel tanks could precipitate a fireball. Far more common, however, was the likelihood of bullets hitting the gas cylinders and causing explosive depressurization and resulting blunt-forces injuries to the operator. Also, the range of a man-portable flamethrower rarely exceeded 25m, so a two-man flamethrower team had to lumber perilously close to their target to deploy the weapon, thus presenting a highly visible target to every Soviet rifleman and submachine-gunner in the vicinity. Needless to say, being a flamethrower operator was not the most popular role within the *Pionier-Bataillon*. (Photo by R. Grimm/PhotoQuest/ Getty Images)

For most of the Soviet riflemen, like those here, the standard weapon was the 7.62mm Mosin-Nagant M1891/30 bolt-action rifle. A basic, hard-wearing and reliable 7.62×54mmR bolt-action weapon, feeding from a five-round internal box magazine, it had much the same combat characteristics as the German Mauser Kar 98k, but was substantially longer, by more than 120mm. The length did not help the rifleman use the weapon in urban combat, but it did mean that the M1891/30 could be easily repurposed as a sniping rifle, with some modification of the bolt handle to allow for fitting an optical sight. Soviet snipers therefore became much feared and respected by German troops, a constant hindrance to any sort of free movement. (AirSeaLand Photos/Cody Images)

two outer packs officially held hand grenades, but could also be repurposed for small demolition charges.

Finally, since World War I the combat engineers had been known for their use of flamethrowers, of which they had four main types – the Flammenwerfer 35, 40, 41 and 42 – each generation offering improvements in either portability, burn time, ignition reliability or range.

Soviet

In many historical accounts, and particularly within the hothouse of opinions on the internet, there is much debate about the logistical situation of the Red Army during the battle of Stalingrad, particularly in relation to the common narrative of Soviet infantry going into battle with just one rifle between two men. This image can be painted too broadly across the Red Army at this time, but it is certainly true that in the initial months of the battle there were some severe problems within Soviet logistics, especially in terms of ammunition and armament supply. As one Red Army communications officer – Tamara Kalmykova of the 64th Army – observed: 'How long will an anti-tank rifle last if it only had six boxes of cartridges? It's no good against two or three hundred tanks. That's why many of our soldiers threw themselves under tanks with grenades – it was sheer desperation. And many of our troops had no proper weapons at all – just a spade and a knife' (quoted in Jones 2014: 30). Given the devastating retreat to Stalingrad, in which Soviet forces had suffered near catastrophic losses, the logistical confusion resulting from mounting the city's defence, and the problems associated with getting supplies across the Volga under the attrition of German artillery and air strikes, it was inevitable that the front-line infantry would suffer shortages of the most essential tools. Yet while some units, particularly those composed of hapless civilian levies or even more condemned men within penal battalions, would always remain shockingly under-resourced, the systems supporting regular infantry divisions eventually recovered. Consequently, most troops went into action reasonably provisioned with weapons and ammunition, although likely never to levels of personal satisfaction.

The standard-issue weapon of the Soviet infantryman was the Mosin-Nagant M1891/30 rifle. Although the Mosin-Nagant provided the ubiquitous firepower of the Red Army, Stalingrad has become heavily associated with the defining Soviet SMG, the 7.62×25mm PPSh-41. Introduced in 1941, this formidable weapon was the ideal weapon for city fighting. It was ultra-reliable, even in sub-zero conditions (aided, of course, by the Red Army's long experience of developing arctic-grade lubricant products and winter oiling techniques). It was mechanically basic, hence could be mass produced easily in non-specialized workshops and small engineering plants, and so it was available in increasingly large quantities from its introduction into the Rifle Division table of organization and equipment (TO&E) in spring 1941. Thus a Soviet rifle brigade TO&E in April 1941 listed a total of 95 SMGs for the entire brigade, including the 33 within the three-platoon dedicated SMG company. By July 1942, however, the brigade SMG allocation had risen to 229 SMGs; a full division had 711 such weapons. At Stalingrad that winter, however, the mass production of the PPSh-41 started to trickle then flood through to the front-line troops, resulting in a high percentage of the troops, and particularly the 'Storm Groups' (see below), taking the SMG into action.

Soviet riflemen move cautiously, using the pile of rubble to shield them from possible German fire. The man on the left appears to have fitted the 508mm M91/30 spike bayonet, an unwieldy weapon for close-quarters fighting, but a useful last resort if ammunition was low. (Photo by PhotoQuest/ Getty Images)

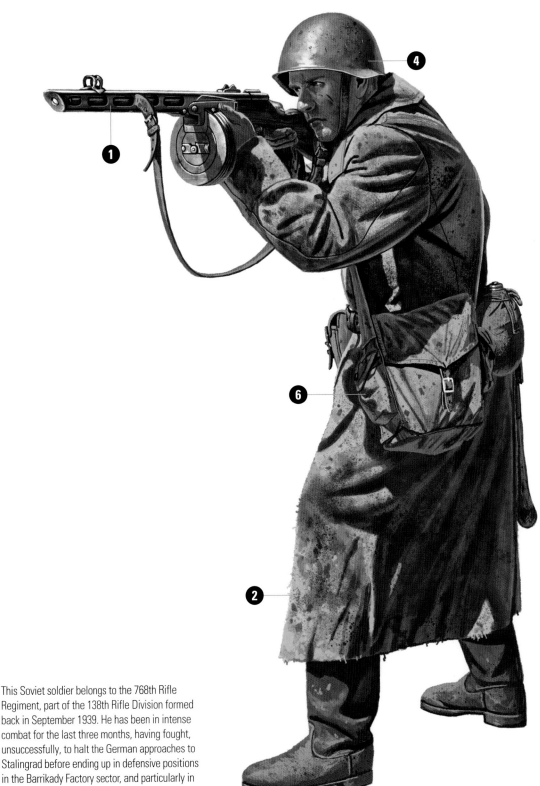

This Soviet soldier belongs to the 768th Rifle Regiment, part of the 138th Rifle Division formed back in September 1939. He has been in intense combat for the last three months, having fought, unsuccessfully, to halt the German approaches to Stalingrad before ending up in defensive positions in the Barrikady Factory sector, and particularly in the workers' housing area.

Weapons, dress and equipment

His firearm is the redoubtable PPSh-41 SMG (**1**). Even with the large capacity of the 71-round drum magazine, the PPSh-41 could empty this quickly with its 900rd/min rate of fire. The soldier would train his trigger finger to squeeze off bursts of 3–5 rounds, with longer bursts for suppressive fire. The maximum effective range of the weapon was about 180m.

With the approach of winter, the temperature in Stalingrad dropped persistently to sub-zero. To protect himself against the cold, this soldier is wearing the buttoned-up *shinel* greatcoat (**2**), made of heavy greyish-brown wool. Not only did this coat shield against the cold, but in Stalingrad it also acted as a form of camouflage when impregnated

with dust, the long coat breaking up the silhouette of the soldier and also blending into the background of rubble. Just visible from beneath the greatcoat are his high leather enlisted man's jackboots (**3**). Head protection comes in the form of an M40 steel helmet (**4**). Like his German counterpart, this rifleman is carrying only light equipment to aid his manoeuvrability in the urban terrain. Hanging on the front of his standard enlisted man's leather belt is a canvas pouch for the PPSh-41's drum magazine (**5**), plus a canvas BN-PN gas mask bag (**6**). To his rear is an entrenching tool (**7**), which when the edge was sharpened also doubled as a useful close-quarters combat tool. A water canteen (**8**) completes his basic equipment.

A group of Soviet soldiers patrol through the ruins of Stalingrad. On an initial glance it is difficult to ascertain whether the soldiers are German or Soviet, as the winter uniforms of both sides could appear similar. Furthermore, we see that the patrol is carrying a mix of weaponry – both an MP 40 and a PPSh-41 are in evidence. (Photo by Laski Diffusion/Getty Images)

Beyond the bolt-action rifle and the SMG, the Soviet rifleman could rely upon support fire from three principal types of machine gun. The standard LMG was the Degtyaryov DP 1928, a 7.62mm weapon firing at 550rd/min from its signature 47-round flat pan magazine (actually its main mechanical weak point). Heavier support fire came from two belt-fed weapons – the 7.62mm Maxim M1910, one of the many direct derivatives of Hiram Maxim's original water-cooled weapon, and the DShK 1938, which fired the hefty 12.7mm (.50-calibre) round. Both of the heavier weapons were on wheeled mounts, which could make them awkward to deploy around the rubble-strewn terrain of Stalingrad, but they were good in defensive positions.

For grenades, the Soviets drew on four types. The M1914/30, RGD-33 and F1 were all fragmentation grenades, of varying design but similar explosive power. The RPG-40, meanwhile, was an anti-tank grenade with a heavier 0.6kg charge and an impact fuse. Although it was effective against lightly armoured vehicles, against more substantial tanks it could inflict little serious damage, although it remained a useful device against German defensive positions.

The Soviets at Stalingrad also made creative use of anti-tank rifles, specifically the Degtyaryov PTRD and Simonov PTRS, both issued in 14.5mm calibre and offering penetration of 25mm of armour (0 degrees) at 500m. The key difference between the two was that the PTRD was a single-shot weapon, while the PTRS was a semi-automatic rifle, with a five-round box magazine. Firing both guns was a duty only for the physically thick-set and mentally resilient. Not only was it imperative to mount the gun properly – not easy in the mental overload of battle – to avoid a broken shoulder or collar bone, but against the new breed of German tanks the 14.5mm rounds had little effect against the thicker armour. Nevertheless, the anti-tank rifles did give the German vehicle crews reason for caution, and the heavy bullets could also be directed against other types of structure, such as walls and barricades.

Three Soviet soldiers aim their PPSh-41s through a window aperture at enemy troops. A group of submachine-gunners together could deliver absolutely ferocious levels of firepower, but they had to be prepared to move before they attracted countering fire from tanks or artillery. The real influence exerted by the PPSh-41 was in the stream of lead it could put on target. It had a rate of fire of around 900rd/min, and could feed from either a 35-round detachable box or a capacious 71-round drum magazine, the latter's capacity meaning reduced reloading downtime. This ferocious firepower, combined with the SMG's total reliability, meant that it was the weapon of choice in Stalingrad, and indeed other Eastern Front city battles. Little wonder that the PPSh-41 is commonly seen in the hands of German soldiers, who eagerly swapped out their rifles or MP 40s for this trusted combat tool. The widespread distribution of the weapon meant that the German forces faced terrifying levels of firepower in almost every clash, firepower that they often could not match on an individual level. (Courtesy of the Central Museum of the Armed Forces, Moscow via Stavka)

TRAINING

German

While the weapon types described above gave the German combat engineers and the Soviet riflemen a roughly even balance of firepower, the same cannot be said for their training. The German *Pioniertruppen* were extremely highly trained individuals. Not only were they often recruited from civilian professions that had a direct relation to their engineering roles – electrical engineers, carpenters, plumbers, factory machine operators, road- and bridge-builders, etc. – but during their formative years they had also received the militarized education so integral to the Third Reich, both in the Hitlerjugend (Hitler Youth) and in the Reichsarbeitsdienst (RAD; Reich Labour Service). The former gave the soldier some military fundamentals, such as handling a

This well-known image shows German troops advancing into the outskirts of Stalingrad. They are heavily laden with individual kit, but during an actual assault they would pare down their kit to pure combat essentials: weapon and ammunition, grenades, water, plus any specialist equipment such as demolition charges (for the combat engineers). (AirSeaLand Photos/Cody Images)

rifle and utilizing small-unit infantry tactics. The Hitler Youth also instilled a martial and disciplined mind-set in the young man, one that was reinforced by the physical labour duties within the RAD.

If recruited into the German Army before 1942, the combat engineer would receive 16 weeks of basic infantry training; the casualties and emergencies of that year, however, necessitated a drop to 12 weeks of basic training. The basic training was that of all German infantry soldiers, from parade-ground drill through to field combat tactics and weapons handling. If they completed this stage effectively, they would receive specialist in-battalion training in all the skills that made them a combat engineer. Gordon Rottman here clarifies something of the spectrum of skills involved:

> In their units over the next months they learned a wide variety of skills from experienced NCOs and officers: erecting various types of barbed-wire entanglements and fences, planting and erecting anti-tank and anti-personnel mines, constructing squad bunkers, machine-gun bunkers and other small fighting positions, use of inflatable boats, assembling pontoon and float bridges, erecting small timber bridges for light vehicles and personnel, building corduroy roads, repairing roads and small bridges, learning how to use hand tools and the limited types of power tools, camouflage techniques, road reconnaissance, rigging electrically and non-electrically initiated demolition charges, and more. (Rottman 2010: 11)

In addition to the in-unit training, the combat engineer might also be sent to a technical school to learn more advanced engineering practices, especially to do with electrical work and advanced construction practices.

Note that what distinguished the German pioneer from a menial sapper was the emphasis on applying his skills to combat situations. So as well as tackling practical challenges in general engineering, the *Pionier* would also practise endless assaults using all the tools of his trade. Particular focus was placed upon position demolition, building assault, flamethrower use and obstacle breaching – all skills that would prove to be highly relevant in Stalingrad. By the time a combat engineer actually went to a front line in 1942, the young man could have more than a decade of paramilitary and professional military training behind him.

Soviet

The situation within the Red Army could not have been more different. Although Stalin had a large reserve of manpower, the fact remained that recruitment had to keep pace with the dizzying levels of losses. In the immediate run-up to Stalingrad, the Red Army had lost nearly 300,000 men in the May Kharkov offensive alone, adding to the millions already killed, wounded or captured since Germany's launch of Operation *Barbarossa* back in June 1941. Thus the training for reservists or new recruits called up to service was little short of parlous, in many cases. It would not be unusual for a Soviet rifleman to go into battle in the Stalingrad maelstrom with little more than one or two weeks of the most basic infantry training. Add this lack of training to that of the many junior officers entering the service, and it is little wonder that the levels of Red Army casualties in Stalingrad were so staggeringly high.

Yet if a Red Army soldier managed to survive, he would benefit from what has been called the 'Stalingrad Academy of Street Fighting'. Through the tactical direction of leaders such as Lieutenant-General Vasily Ivanovich Chuikov, commander of the 62nd Army, the Red Army did develop tactical doctrine and method in Stalingrad (see below), and this trickled through to the front-line soldiery and fused with hard-won battlefield experience.

The Red Army also made some investment in training soldiers in specialist combat techniques, although again much of this was conducted in-unit in 'live' combat zones. For example, a US War Department analysis of the Red Army in 1942 observed how the 'automatic rifleman' – the Soviet soldier armed with an SMG – was given a rounded instruction in assault tactics and general infantry skills:

The PTRD anti-tank rifle shown here was a formidable weapon to fire, as it had a 14.5mm calibre and little sophistication in terms of recoil handling, apart from the large muzzle brake at the front. The Soviets made effective use of anti-tank rifles during the battle of Stalingrad, even disabling battle tanks by targeting thinner top and rear armour. (Photo by Laski Diffusion/ Getty Images)

According to a Russian instructional poster, best results are obtained with this weapon as follows: single shot, up to about 300 yards [274m]; short bursts, about 200 yards [183m]; long bursts, about 100 yards [91m] … The program of training for automatic riflemen is drawn up with special consideration as to their battle functions. The individual training of the automatic riflemen approximates that of the infantry riflemen in the elementary stages. Emphasis is placed on the following: (a) Thorough familiarity with the automatic rifle, to include reduction of stoppages and care in the field; (b) Marksmanship, to include firing from all positions at stationary, moving, and surprise targets; (c) Throwing of grenades and gasoline bottles, especially against tanks, embrasures, and trenches; (d) Ability to ski; (e) Self-orientation by azimuth, compass, or map at any time. In the individual tactical training of automatic riflemen, 8 to 10 hours are devoted to courses in: 'The Automatic Rifleman in Offense,' 'Actions of Automatic Riflemen in Attack and Inside the Enemy Defenses' and 'The Automatic Rifleman in Defense.' Stress is laid upon movement by rushes and crawling noiseless approach to enemy positions, use of camouflage, and utilization of cover. Each trainee must learn the various means of preparing satisfactory fire positions for prone, kneeling, sitting, and standing fox holes. He must also know how to fire from skis and tanks. (US War Department 1942)

Although in-combat training is one of the hardest, and most costly, forms of military instruction, there is no doubt that the Red Army became reasonably good at it, although often only through a hardened attitude to the lives of their soldiery. Thus although the German soldier often felt that he was superior individually to the Soviet rifleman, he never disrespected his opponent's fighting ability or tenacity.

TACTICS

The tactical context of the battle of Stalingrad was street fighting, pure and simple. Although both sides utilized air power, artillery and armour heavily and significantly in combat, ultimately the taking and holding of Stalingrad's streets and buildings depended upon the infantry fighting at close quarters.

It must be remembered that neither side actively sought out urban warfare. City combat is by its very nature unpredictable, extremely costly in terms of men and *matériel*, and time-consuming, hence the pre-war doctrine of both the German Army and the Soviet Army emphasized bypassing urban centres in favour of mobile warfare. The psychological salience placed upon the city of Stalingrad by both Hitler and Stalin, however, meant that the combatants had to embrace street fighting to its fullest extent.

German

The tactics of the German combat engineers cannot be studied entirely in isolation from the other units that they supported, or those from which they received support. In offensive actions, the Germans at Stalingrad relied as much as possible upon preparatory air strikes (given some measure of precision by using the Ju 87 Stuka dive-bomber as a form of aerial artillery) and tanks and assault guns to provide moving cover and also the firepower to blast apart any strongpoints. Mortar batteries and heavy machine guns delivered constant suppressive fire.

One of the World War I innovations brought back into play at Stalingrad was that of the 'storm detachment', small units of about ten men, heavily equipped with demolitions and small arms and tasked with taking a localized target. One of the best descriptions of how this worked, at least in the initial stages of the Stalingrad offensive, comes from a German officer, whose words made it into a 1943 US military report entitled 'Tactics of Street Fighting on the Russian Front':

> The attacking German troops move forward behind tanks and assault guns, sweep away barricades with gun fire, knock holes into house-walls, and crush down wire obstacles. Guns and mortars batter concealed positions, antitank guns cover the side streets against possible flanking operations by tanks, antiaircraft guns are ready to meet attacking aircraft. Low-flying aircraft and Stukas attack the rear sections of resistance in the inner town, and the supply points and routes inside the town. Machine guns engage snipers on the roofs. Covered thus, infantry and engineer assault detachments, keeping close to the walls, advance over the wreckage from street to street, break down blocked doors and cellar windows with explosive charges and grenades, smoke out the less accessible corners with flame-throwers, and comb houses from ground floor to roof. In all this, they have frequently to engage the enemy in hand-to-hand fighting. (Quoted in US War Department 1943)

The fluency achieved by the Germans, including by the combat engineers, in these assault tactics, combined with the unpreparedness of the Red Army defenders, is testified to by the bloody progress they made in

Hunkered down for fear of Soviet snipers, a German assault team moves forward. The soldier on the right rear has an MG 34 tripod on his back; the tripod was set up when the assault team wanted sustained and accurate support fire. (AirSeaLand Photos/Cody Images)

August–November 1942, which squeezed the Soviet troops into small pockets of defence on the western bank of the Volga. Yet the report accurately goes on to state how the offensive momentum bled out of the German units, after which combat devolved to intense rolling small-unit actions:

> These assaults failed to make much progress, partly due to the great quantity of artillery concentrated by the Russians, and partly due to the way in which the large number of reinforced concrete and stone buildings were adapted by the Russians for defense, even when they were in a ruined condition. The Germans were virtually forced to give up large-scale tank attacks as being too costly, and the fighting reverted to intense street fighting between relatively small infantry and engineer assault groups, liberally supplied with flamethrowers. (US War Department 1943)

As will become evident in the battle accounts in this study, the German combat engineers' knowledge of building structures, the physical properties of defensive positions, and their understanding of demolitions and flamethrowers, meant that they could formulate the optimal combination of weaponry and manoeuvre tactics to uproot dogged Soviet defenders from shattered and complicated positions. The key qualities for a successful assault were then, as now, maintaining an aggressive tempo, limiting casualty levels, innovative avenues of approach, and honed room and building clearance procedures.

Soviet

During the early stages of the Stalingrad battle, the Red Army often resorted to horribly costly frontal assault tactics, in which hundreds of men were mown down running blindly across open spaces. Chuikov, as commander of the Stalingrad defenders, quickly realized that this tactical profligacy would not win the battle, and important measures filtered down to the front line from his headquarters. The most famous of these innovations was that of 'hugging' the enemy, staying within 50m of the Germans to obviate their application of aerial bombardment and artillery fire. It was this measure, more than any other, which turned Stalingrad into a close-quarters cauldron.

Yet the Red Army infantry also refined their defensive tactics considerably to impose far higher costs upon attacking Germans. The secret to the Soviet defence was its multi-dimensional aspect. Individual strongpoints were heavily reinforced physically and humanly, with every room, floor, window and pile of rubble turned into a position for active all-round defence. Supplies of ammunition, food and water would be stockpiled, to enable the strongpoint to endure repeated attacks without resupply. Crucially, however, multiple strongpoints were linked through command relationships (several buildings might have a single headquarters coordinating their fire), communication trenches and interlocking fields of fire, the latter including anti-tank guns (when available) and often tanks dug-in as fixed gun emplacements. Such

Soviet troops take up firing positions among the ruins of a factory plant. Note how each of them appears to be armed with the PPSh-41; SMGs were issued in increasingly high numbers from late 1942 as a way of boosting small-unit firepower. (AirSeaLand Photos/Cody Images)

Artillery played a critical role in the eventual Soviet victory at Stalingrad, inflicting constant attrition on the Germans. Here we see 152mm ML-20 howitzers, positioned on the eastern bank of the Volga and firing across the river into the city. (AirSeaLand Photos/Cody Images)

strongpoint arrangements created a tenacious defence-in-depth that drove the German attackers mad with their obstinacy.

The Soviet infantry also developed greater efficiency in offensive tactics. Like the German storm detachments, Soviet 'storm groups' were formed with a similar operational outlook. These groups were divided into three elements: assault groups, reinforcement groups, and reserve groups. Chuikov himself later explained the composition and tactical purpose of each of these elements:

Assault group(s): Their job was to break in and take the building. Each assault group had 6–8 men with submachine guns, 5–12 grenades ('pocket artillery'), knives and sharpened spades; collectively these were always under a single commander.

Reinforcement group(s): Once the commander of the assault groups signalled 'We're in', the reinforcement groups would move in from different directions. Once inside they would capture firing positions, set up, then block any attempted enemy interference from outside. Given their role this group had machine guns, submachine guns, mortars, anti-tank rifles and guns, crow-bars, picks and explosives. They often included sappers and snipers. The reinforcement group(s) came under the command of the commander of the storm group. The machine gunners, anti-tank riflemen and mortar gunners entered the building first. Their assistants followed with ammunition and food for one day. The men occupied the centre and upper floors to cover the approaches to the building. Once established they occupied further firing points in front of and on the flanks of the building. When the building was in their possession they entrenched, adapted existing fortifications, built new ones, and dug communication trenches.

Reserve group(s): These formed the basis of new assault groups, prevented enemy attacks from the flanks, and if necessary, blocked any counter-attacks. (Chuikov 1963)

The dynamic similarities with the German offensive tactics are notable. Where the Soviets innovated was often in the timing and tempo of their attacks. Night-time assaults were common, launched by surprise without any preparatory fire, and German survivors remember the nights as one of the most fearful and disorientating periods of the daily cycle. The operational pressure imposed upon the Germans was also locally relentless, adding attrition at the psychological level as well as in terms of casualties inflicted. What is also important to note is that the assault groups were not purely composed of Red Army riflemen, but also contained groups of sappers – essentially combat engineers – as demolition specialists to support each assault. The sappers would also be proficient in converting captured territory into a defensive strongpoint.

The Soviet infantry at Stalingrad became hardened street fighters, but their lives still tended to be short and brutal. As both sides learned the skills of urban combat, and honed them to a high degree, the battle became as much about tenacity, attrition and survival as it did about front-line tactics.

A Red Army flamethrower operator sends out a jet of oily flame from his ROKS flamethrower into the ruins of Stalingrad. The flamethrower had utility for flushing out obstinate defenders from well-fortified positions, although the restricted movement of the operators meant their lives could be short on a fast-moving battlefield. (AirSeaLand Photos/Cody Images)

Assault towards the Tractor Factory

14–15 October 1942

BACKGROUND TO BATTLE

From September 1942 until the beginning of November, 6. Armee and 4. Panzerarmee fought brutally for every square metre of gain in the struggle for Stalingrad. The soldiers of Chuikov's 62nd Army, mounting a desperate defence, managed to inflict terrible casualties upon the German forces, but nevertheless found themselves pressed back into an ever-shrinking perimeter on the west bank of the Volga, with less than 10 per cent of the city in their

This German soldier is one of the many who opted to replace his service weapon with a Soviet PPSh-41. As well as offering a higher degree of reliability than the German SMGs (particularly in sub-zero temperatures or very dirty conditions), the PPSh-41 also had a higher magazine capacity and a faster rate of fire. (AirSeaLand Photos/ Cody Images)

hands. Yet still they held on, fuelled by a constant flow of men and *matériel* across the Volga, the crossings literally made under the guns of the Germans.

Following the aerial bombardment of Stalingrad on 23 August, and the continuing bombardment from that date, virtually the whole of Stalingrad had been transformed into a rubble-strewn wilderness of gaunt streets and gutted buildings, devastated but actually ideal for mounting a defence, as 6. Armee discovered to its cost between 14 September and 14 October. Two major offensive efforts to capture the city, particularly in the northern industrial sectors, made progress during this time, but only with agonizing cost in lives and *matériel*. On 14 October it was time for a third attempt, and our first battle to study.

Here our focus is sharply on one unit involved in this action, Pionier-Bataillon 305, the standing combat-engineer battalion within 305. Infanterie-Division. Together with 389. Infanterie-Division and 14. Panzer-Division, Pionier-Bataillon 305 was part of a dedicated assault group termed Gruppe *Jaenecke*, commanded by the eponymous Generalleutnant Erwin Jaenecke. For the offensive, Gruppe *Jaenecke* was to drive into the Factory District and capture the Brickworks and the Dzerzhinsky Tractor Factory, pushing through to reach the Volga and secure the left flank for the offensive, before swinging south and driving down the river in a progressive clearance operation, accompanied by 14. Panzer-Division.

The three companies of combat engineers that comprised Pionier-Bataillon 305 were allocated as spear-tip assault units to assist the infantry of 305. Infanterie-Division, a position of terrible vulnerability. 2./PiBtl 305 had something of a reprieve, however, when it was moved into a more subordinate attacking role in support of Infanterie-Regiment 576. (The other principal 305. Infanterie-Division unit involved in the attack was Infanterie-Regiment 578.) By 0200hrs on 14 October, the German combat engineers and their infantry counterparts were finally ready, positioned on the high ground west of the industrial area. Each company, and each platoon, had a clear sense of their objectives, the complex battlefront rationalized with grid-sector numbers. H-Hour was 0730hrs.

This grainy image of Soviet troops fighting in the Factory District illustrates the complexities of the terrain faced by those fighting in the area. Facing Pionier-Bataillon 305 on 14–15 October were three battered Soviet rifle divisions (37th Guards, 95th and 112nd) plus, to the north, the 124th and 149th Rifle brigades. Although all these Soviet formations had significantly reduced manpower, the Red Army riflemen still retained the advantage of excellent positioning in the ruined buildings. On the downside, the fact that the Soviet troops occupied readily identifiable positions meant that those positions were hammered constantly by aerial and artillery bombardment. (AirSeaLand Photos/Cody Images)

MAP KEY

1 **0730hrs, 14 October:** I./IR 576, supported by two companies of mechanized artillery, makes a powerful attack up through the sectors in front and to the north-west of the Sports Stadium, overcoming resistance from 2/109th GRR and taking the high ground (Sector 16) on the northern flank of the offensive. This push serves to protect the main drives forward from Soviet flanking fire.

2 **c.0800hrs, 14 October:** The rest of Infanterie-Regiment 576 plus Infanterie-Regiment 578 push directly towards the Sports Stadium, aiming at the boundary between the 109th and 114th Guards Rifle regiments. Combat-engineer companies of Pionier-Bataillon 305 support the attacks, with 2. and 3./PiBtl 305 supporting Infanterie-Regiment 576 and 1./PiBtl 305 supporting Infanterie-Regiment 578.

3 **c.0900hrs, 14 October:** 1./PiBtl 305 and elements from Infanterie-Regiment 578 eliminate a Soviet bunker complex in front of the multi-storey houses behind the Stadium. The German advance is under heavy fire from the buildings as it moves forward, and 3./PiBtl 305 becomes embroiled in intense street fighting.

4 **c.1100hrs, 14 October:** II. and III./IR 576 take the Sports Stadium from the 109th Guards Rifle Regiment,

opening the way for the Germans to push through towards the industrial zone. Infanterie-Regiment 578 assaults down Kultarmeiskaya Street, while Infanterie-Regiment 576 pushes towards Mokraya Mechetka Street to the north, engaging in horrendous street fighting.

5 **1500hrs, 14 October:** With pioneers in support, Infanterie-Regiment 576 reaches Mokraya Mechetka Street, having suffered horrendous casualties along the way. The surviving soldiers of the 524th Rifle Regiment dig in on the defensive.

6 **1700hrs, 14 October:** An attack by the 385th Rifle Regiment from positions on the Mechetka River threatens the German hold on the Sports Stadium. It is halted by German firepower, but it does succeed in stopping the German advance in Sector 12, in the northern part of the battlefield.

7 **Night of 14/15 October:** Infanterie-Regimenter 576 and 578 conduct numerous house- and building-clearance operations, supported by all three companies of Pionier-Bataillon 305. The Tractor Factory is fully taken by the Germans, with capture of the northern part assigned to Infanterie-Regiment 578, with 1. and 3./PiBtl 305 in support. The Germans encounter very heavy resistance, however, in Sectors 18 and 23, to the north-east of the Factory District.

Battlefield environment

Much of the German offensive of 14–15 October 1942 began from open elevated ground west of the main industrial area, a launch point that gave the *Pioniere* good visibility of the battlefield in front of them. Yet the approaches to the main Soviet positions included large areas of open land, pock-marked with low-lying Soviet defensive positions, but also flanked by firing points from nearby housing and other buildings. This combination of open ground and flanking positions meant that the terrain rather favoured the defender, although conversely the Germans also had clear fields of fire for their armour and

artillery. The built-up areas presented the familiar challenges of urban warfare. The street areas were regimented in layout, often being based on a block/grid system, although the devastation caused by the fighting meant that rubble and collapsed buildings still made movement a challenge. A special feature of the battlefield was the Sports Stadium building, by 14 October a wrecked structure featuring large areas of collapsed spectator seating, in which the Soviet defenders could position themselves almost unseen. Weather on the day was clear and sunny in the morning, with cloud increasing as the day wore on.

Two unfortunate German horses, killed by artillery fire, lie rotting in the streets of Stalingrad. The background of this image shows how the wrecked city featured areas of intense close-quarters urban fighting, but combined with open spaces that acted as lethal killing zones for attackers. (Nik Cornish at Stavka)

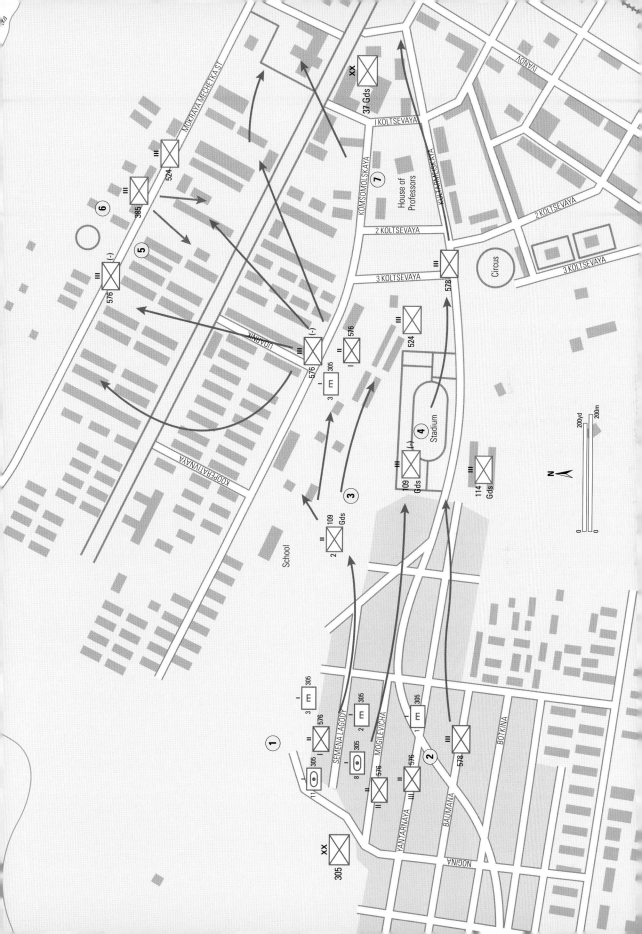

INTO COMBAT

For the Soviet troops within the industrial district, the first searing indication that they were about to face a major attack came at 0400hrs, when a huge preliminary bombardment was unleashed across the front by massed German artillery of every description, from light mortars through to heavy howitzers and rocket-launchers. Then, at 0645hrs, wave upon wave of Ju 87 Stuka dive-bombers also began to add their contribution, avoiding the nearby German positions, which were identified with aerial marker flags. One Soviet officer remembered the hell of those hours:

> On the morning of 14 October it was no longer possible to see the sun, only a sad brown circlet, peeping through the clouds. Spumes of earth, fire and smoke rose up around us. It was not possible to hear the sound of the individual shooting anymore – there was just a rolling, thunderous wall of noise. Sitting in one's trench – in the midst of this uproar – you felt that no-one could be left alive, either around you or behind you, that everything was being consumed in this terrible bombardment. (Quoted in Jones 2014: 201)

A German soldier clambers across collapsed metal fabrication in the Factory District. One of the unnerving consequences of there being so much ruined metalwork in the factory fighting was the constant ricochets, creating unpredictable lines of fire. Swift movement by foot was almost impossible inside the factories, and it was often difficult to get a clear line of sight on the enemy. It should be noted that the combat engineers, like the Soviet troops they faced, were not up to strength. 305. Infanterie-Division and its combat-engineer battalion had fought a long campaign across southern Russia to reach Stalingrad, taking casualties along the way. The aforementioned 2./PiBtl 305, led by Oberleutnant Richard Grimm, was down to about 90 men; the ideal on-paper strength was about double that figure. Furthermore, the combat engineers took additional casualties from Soviet artillery – fired from across the Volga – even as they moved up to their assault positions on 13 October. (AirSeaLand Photos/Cody Images)

At 0730hrs, the units and formations of Gruppe *Jaenecke*, with the combat engineers to the fore, moved out of their positions and into the attack. In the immediate assault, I./IR 576 assaulted positions in Sector 16, overcoming troops from 2/109th GRR to secure the left flank of the main German assault. Soon after Sector 16 was secure, the main forces of Infanterie-Regimenter 576 and 578 surged forward. Their immediate objective was the blasted remnants of the Sports Stadium to the west of the Tractor Factory. Facing them were elements of the 109th and 114th Guards Rifle regiments, backed by the 524th Rifle Regiment. The attackers had some advantages on their side, not least the downward slope of the terrain, which aided more rapid assault movement, and the precision control of air and artillery assets. But the Red Army riflemen had positional advantages, and the attackers ran into a

rippling hail of small-arms fire, plus showers of hand grenades, mortar rounds and artillery shells.

The combat engineers were in the vanguard of this action. As an example, a heavily defended bunker, occupied by troops of the 524th Rifle Regiment, stood in the way of the advancing II./IR 578. The 524th Rifle Regiment was a veteran unit; it had fought, as part of the 112th Rifle Division, 16th Army, during the battle for Moscow, back in December 1941–February 1942, and had been in action ever since. For the Germans, the bunker had to be cleared otherwise the advance could not proceed, and it fell to 1./PiBtl 305 to take it out. The company was commanded by Oberleutnant Heinz Schaate, an Eastern Front veteran who had taken charge on 22 August 1942. The actual job of taking the bunker was given to 3. Zug, led by a Feldwebel Grosskreutz, the specific assault component being 8. Gruppe under Gefreiter Hermann Heeb. Under heavy covering fire the assault team worked their way progressively forward, using any scraps of dead ground available, interspersed with assault rushes. The Soviet defenders maintained a withering fire in response, even as the bunker apertures were chipped and blasted by incoming bullets. Eventually, the combat engineers closed the distance, and a satchel charge was posted through an aperture, destroying the bunker and its occupants when it detonated. This smallest of actions, repeated hundreds of times up and down the front, cost 8. Gruppe two men killed, both experienced soldiers.

With the bunker cleared, the combat engineers joined the general movement forward of 305. Infanterie-Division, which now inched into the avenues and high buildings surrounding the shattered Sports Stadium, which was also in Soviet hands. 3./PiBtl 305 was soon locked in dreadful house-to-house fighting, the Soviet riflemen fully utilizing the bewildering array of firing angles to impose maximum inertia on the attacking forces. Meanwhile, 2./PiBtl 305 divided its platoons to support attacking battalions of Infanterie-Regiment 576, with II./IR 576 and III./IR 576 pushing directly down onto the Sports Stadium, aided by heavy support from armour. The main opposition there came from the 109th Guards Rifle Regiment, part

Street fighting, western Factory District

German view: Soldiers from 3./PiBtl 305 attempt to take the large apartment blocks beyond the Sports Stadium during the attack of 14 October 1942, and meet heavy resistance in the process. The time is the early morning, just after dawn on what was a clear and sunny day, but already the air is choked with the dust and smoke of battle. To provide cover to comrades making an advance up the left of the street, an MG 34 team puts down heavy fire, using the green light of the tracers to guide the impacts from window to window. The assistant gunner is quickly opening another box of 250 rounds of belted ammunition; high ammunition consumption was a problem for both sides in Stalingrad. At the same time as the machine-gunner lays down fire, a flamethrower operator with a Flammenwerfer 35 looks for an opportune moment to advance into the attack, although the weight of the flamethrower and his lack of small arms makes him a vulnerable target for Soviet snipers. Note also that the combat engineers have some armour support, in the form of a PzKpfw IV Ausf E, but this has been disabled by anti-tank rifle fire from the building ahead.

Soviet view: Riflemen from the 109th Guards Rifle Regiment put up a trenchant defence against the German attack on 14 October. Every window, doorway, staircase, corridor, alleyway and street was turned into a defensive position. Here this group of men have chosen a second-floor window to give them a broad 'kill zone' over the street below. The team brings together a mix of firepower. Automatic fire is provided by the PPSh-41 SMGs. The figure just off-centre is changing out one of the 71-round drum magazines; the high capacity of these magazine was a welcome resource during the Stalingrad street fighting, although the magazines took a long while to refill once empty. The man on the right is firing the standard Mosin-Nagant 1891/30 rifle. On the other side of the room, however, the man is armed with a 14.5mm PTRD anti-tank rifle. He has already disabled a German tank with his accurate shots, hitting the engine compartment as the tank presented itself from the side when turning into the street. Although the Soviet defenders shown here are holding their own, they must decide soon whether to move positions before the weight of fire through the window becomes too great.

of the 37th Guards Rifle Division, itself created on 2 August 1942 from the personnel of the 1st Airborne Corps. Being airborne soldiers, the Soviet troops put up a hardened resistance, but steadily the tank guns and the demolition charges from the combat engineers knocked out their positions one by one.

Having reached and suppressed the Sports Stadium, the German attack now split into two thrusts, one element (Infanterie-Regiment 578) heading down Kultarmeiskaya Street directly behind the stadium and down Ivanov Street, closing on Kultarmeiskaya Street at a 45-degree angle, while the other element (Infanterie-Regiment 576) pushed out towards Mokraya Mechetka Street further to the north. Every building, every undulation in the ground, every pile of rubble, was viciously contested. Previously innocuous buildings became horrifying killing grounds. A large school building, occupied by soldiers of the 37th Guards Rifle Division and used as an artillery spotting post, put up hours of resistance at a heavy cost in lives on both sides. The diaries of the combat engineers list a growing catalogue of dead and wounded from within their ranks, some of the wounded succumbing to their injuries in field hospitals, which were overwhelmed by the levels of casualties mounting up. Eventually, by around 1500hrs, Infanterie-Regiment 576 had managed to reach Mokraya Mechetka Street and secure all of its Sector 13 objectives. The regiment then advanced to take most of Sector 11 and Sector 12, by which time the momentum was starting to bleed out of the attack.

The situation for the Soviet defenders was, by this time, parlous. Subsequent after-action reports of the 37th Guards Rifle Division were honest about their defensive collapse and about the attackers' deft handling of multi-arms cooperation between artillery, armour, air power and infantry. Some highlights of the report are illustrative, not only for explaining the events of 14–15 October but also the preceding context to the battle:

Here a German unit advances in cooperation with a StuG III assault gun, the infantry providing the armour with protection against anti-tank opponents, the armour providing the infantry with heavy firepower for position destruction. It must be remembered that at Stalingrad, the German combat engineers were just one strand – albeit an important one – of a true combined-arms offensive. Infantry, Panzer troops, artillerymen and combat engineers fought together shoulder to shoulder, the footsoldiers moving alongside a total of 300 tanks and assault guns massed for the entire offensive. The ground assault was coordinated constantly with air and artillery power, the artillery making progressive 50m shifts forward of the advance, while forward observers communicated with the predatory Ju 87 Stuka dive-bombers overhead, which made constant peeling attacks. (AirSeaLand Photos/ Cody Images)

German infantry, plus what appear to be (by their hats) some auxiliary troops, advance behind an assault gun through the ruins of Stalingrad. This viewpoint shows the main area targeted by Soviet anti-tank riflemen – the rear engine compartment, where armour was at its thinnest. (AirSeaLand Photos/Cody Images)

OPPOSITE
Soviet riflemen engage in intense street fighting. One of the men is climbing up onto the next floor, probably with the intention of crossing through the building to deliver fire from a higher vantage point. (Photo by ullstein bild/ullstein bild via Getty Images)

1. By the beginning of the Germans' decisive offensive, the division's units were worn down by prolonged fighting, having suffered significant losses in personnel and equipment. In addition, after the division's [previous] night offensive, it had just begun to dig in along the positions it reached, and the defensive works were not completed by the time the Germans began their offensive. The incomplete work in preparing foxholes along the forward edge and the unsuitability of the local measures for constructing firing points in the sector of the 114th and 118th Gds. RR hindered the conduct of combat by these units.
[…]
3. The division suffered heavy losses in personnel and weapons while repelling the frenzied enemy attacks. We are experiencing shortages of antitank shells for the artillery. The antitank means remaining in the division are not enough to withstand a massive attack by tanks echeloned in depth. More than 20 enemy tanks have been destroyed along the forward edge and up to a battalion of infantry have been destroyed. The struggle is going on for every metre, and the infantry, before being cut off behind every charred wreck from the first echelon of tanks, is being supported by a new wave of tanks along the division's entire front. (Quoted in Glantz & House 2009b: 780–81)

Despite the general advance of the German forces on 14 October, the tenacity of the Soviet infantrymen was still remarkable. Despite the heavy losses incurred, some regiments even managed to mount defiant but ultimately pointless counter-attacks. For example, around 1700hrs a force of some 80 men of the 385th Rifle Regiment made a spirited assault out from positions on the Mechetka River towards the Germans in the Sports Stadium. The

assault force was blown apart by German firepower, but sufficed to bring the German push in Sector 12 to a halt. Meanwhile, the pioneers and other infantry from 305. Infanterie-Division and 389. Infanterie-Division continued to fight hard for the rest of the day, clearing out key sectors of the front line. Beyond 305. Infanterie-Division's sectors, other German forces were making good progress.

Night eventually arrived in Stalingrad, but it did not bring quiet to the battlefield (it rarely did throughout the entire campaign). The Soviet defenders had clearly been outgunned and outmanoeuvred, and had suffered terrible casualties during the day's fighting – the 62nd Army had lost an estimated 10,000 men, against 538 fatalities on the German side, an astonishing disparity partly down to the effective German use of combat engineers – but as always, the Soviet troops were still in the fight. The distinctive H-shaped building called the House of Professors, set between Komsomolskaya Street and Kultarmeiskaya Street, was actually, unbeknown to the Germans, the command post of the 109th Guards Rifle Regiment and the 4th Battalion, 149th Rifle Brigade. As it had simply been bypassed and isolated it remained operational until well into the night, when the occupiers finally attempted to slip away, although they took many casualties in a subsequent gun battle when they were discovered. Reinforcements were also on the way, in the form of the 138th Rifle Division, which even as the German offensive began on 14 October was being prepared to move over the Volga to boost the 62nd Army.

During the night, Infanterie-Regiment 576 conducted a bitter clearance operation of the major apartment complexes in the area. Again, the combat engineers proved of critical value, working closely in combined demolition and flamethrower teams. When a point of resistance was identified, it was pounded with fire to suppress the defenders, allowing the combat engineers to approach closely. Then demolition packs or shaped charges were used either to blow up the enemy directly, or to blast an entry point into the occupied room; the assault team then sprayed the room with small-arms fire or a half-second blast from a flamethrower. If going through a door, grenades always preceded the entry.

The continuing operations on the night of 14/15 October resulted in further gains for the Germans. Further south, 14. Panzer-Division had been able to strike through and hold the southern portion of the Tractor Factory, while Panzergrenadier-Regiment 103 pushed through to the Volga. Yet the momentum of the attack had to be maintained, and at 0700hrs, after 30 minutes of concerted bombing by the Luftwaffe, the offensive resumed in full force. Although the southern part of the Tractor Factory was in German hands, it was a large complex, and capture of the northern part was assigned to Infanterie-Regiment 578, with 1./PiBtl 305 and 3./PiBtl 305 in support.

This day was to be different from the previous one. In a moment of sound command, Chuikov had actually withdrawn many of his troops back to a more defensible line, although isolated groups of Soviets meant that the German troops still had to be wary. In two hours, however, the remainder of the Tractor Factory was captured. Similarly, Grimm's combat engineers, in support of Infanterie-Regiment 576, had a relatively straightforward time occupying workers' settlements in Sector 12, Sector 11 and areas of ground to the north of Sector 14 and Sector 11 (Mark 2013: 360). But clearance operations later in the day ran into some tough resistance from isolated, and often suicidally brave, Soviet groups. In relation to operations in support of Infanterie-Regiment 578 in and around Sector 23 and Sector 18, Mark notes that:

> Schaate's company supported one infantry battalion during its task to capture Section 23 (a cluster of buildings north-east of the Tractor Factory) and straighten out the point between the Volga and Orlovka Brook. Proof that resistance was tougher is found in the fact that Schaate's 1. Kompanie gained a *Sturmtag* for this day ('Attack on Block 23') and at least three of his men were killed ... many more were wounded. (Mark 2013: 362)

Meanwhile, 3./PiBtl 305 fought to clear a block of houses above the Tractor Factory.

Although 14–15 October had been an apparent success for the German offensive, the Soviets continued to demonstrate a relentlessly exhausting counter-response. Much of Infanterie-Regiment 578 was moved north of the captured factory, alongside Infanterie-Regiment 576, occupying high ground and fighting hard to repulse Soviet counter-attacks from across the river valley. This fighting was quite different from that preceding it, and the combat engineers had to shift quickly from their assault mentality to a defensive one. The fact remained that on many levels, the combat engineers had been integral to two days of operational success for the Germans.

The Barrikady Gun Factory

11 November 1942

BACKGROUND TO BATTLE

By 1 November, a month and a half of vicious street fighting in Stalingrad seemed to have brought the Germans close to victory. The city-centre sectors in the south had been captured, as had half the Mamaev Kurgan. Much of the Factory District already lay in German hands, and the 62nd Army was squeezed hard up against the western bank of the Volga. With winter now firmly set in, and 6. Armee reeling against appalling losses – most companies were down to a strength of about 40–50 men, and one division, 94. Infanterie-Division, had an effective strength of fewer than 550 men – the momentum now bled out of the German offensive. Hitler sought to jump-start the attack and take the obdurate city.

The first major German operation of November 1942 would be an attempt, once and for all, to clear the Barrikady and Red October sectors. Facing the Germans were a ragged collection of Soviet rifle divisions, reeling from weeks of incessant fighting. Within and around the Red October Factory were the 39th and 284th Rifle divisions, the latter holding the workers' housing area. The 10 per cent of the Barrikady Gun Factory that remained in Soviet hands was held by men from the 138th, 244th and 308th Rifle divisions, with the workers' housing areas there principally defended by the 768th Rifle Regiment, again of the 138th Rifle Division.

In an attempt to make the offensive decisive, the Germans decided they needed specialist troops at the spearhead. On 2 November, General der Infanterie Kurt Zeitzler (Chief of the OKH General Staff) put forward a

plan to Hitler, responding to suggestions from the commander of Luftflotte 4, Generaloberst Wolfram Freiherr von Richthofen. The intention was to reinforce 305. Infanterie-Division and 379. Infanterie-Division with five combat-engineer battalions, which would lead the way in the assaults into the well-defended sectors. It was felt that the combat engineers' skills in demolitions and fortified position assault were exactly what was needed to break the deadlock. Surrounding this push would be further offensive actions by LI. Armeekorps, consisting of 71., 79., 100. and 295. Infanterie-Divisionen and 14. and 24. Panzer-Divisionen.

Commanding the combat-engineer forces was Major Josef Linden, the 38-year-old commander of Pionier-Bataillon 672, and head of the combat-engineer training school. At his disposal, he was given command of a total of eight combat-engineer battalions: 41, 45 (mot.), 50 (mot.), 162, 294, 305, 336 and 389. On paper, the combat-engineer forces and the other units deployed, including a substantial armoured element, looked formidable. In reality, many of the battalions had already suffered scything losses on the approaches to and within Stalingrad, being reduced to little more than company-strength units. Five of the combat-engineer battalions (45, 50, 162, 294 and 336) were relatively fresh formations, brought in from the rear areas to provide a fresh impetus. The other units were rather battle-worn, and had depleted strength. Pionier-Bataillon 305 and Pionier-Bataillon 398, for example, were at 30 per cent and 50 per cent reduced strength respectively. In total, Linden had about 1,750 men for his forthcoming offensive, but given the strength of the opposition, that scarcely seemed adequate to the task.

The overall plan for the offensive by LI. Armeekorps, eventually scheduled for 11 November, went through several permutations before it settled just prior to the attack date. At first the principal objective was to take out the Soviet salient around the Lazur Chemical Factory, a large and stubborn objective. Stalingrad was a complex battlescape, however, and the pros and cons of Operation *Hubertus* (as it was known) were debated at the highest level. Then, late in the evening of 6 November, Paulus received the following message from Heeresgruppe B:

Franz Müller

A fascinating character to emerge, partially, from the battle of Stalingrad was one Obergefreiter Franz Müller. Details of his early life are virtually non-existent, but we do know that he was born in Upper Franconia and that he was the father of no fewer than seven children. We also understand that he had been sent to 2./PiBtl 305 as a replacement soldier with disciplinary issues hanging over his head – he had been sentenced to 'probation at the front' as punishment for past offences, and he apparently still attracted criticism from his commanders and NCOs.

Nevertheless, Müller served with some distinction as part of a flamethrower team during the Stalingrad battles in November, with Pionier-Bataillon 294 as well as Pionier-Bataillon 305. On one occasion, on 11 November, Müller went underground on his own with a flamethrower, and systematically cleared a street's worth of sewers with his weapon. Müller apparently survived the battle of Stalingrad, but he would not survive the war – he was killed fighting in Italy, possibly while serving with 305. Infanterie-Division at Monte Cassino.

> The Führer has ordered the following: before resuming the attack to capture the Lazur Chemical Factory, the two sections of the city still held by the enemy east of the gun factory and east of the steel factory are to be taken. Only after the bank of the Volga there is entirely in our hands will the assault on the Chemical Factory begin. (Quoted in Mark 2006: 57)

Operation *Hubertus* was annulled, but in its place the combat engineers, infantry and Panzer forces had a new series of objectives. In broad outline, 305. Infanterie-Division and the southern wing of 389. Infanterie-Division were to strike out from positions in the Factory District and drive through to the Volga, taking the remnants of the Barrikady Gun Factory and key objectives such as the Apotheke (Chemist) building and fortress-like Kommissarhaus (Commissar's House) on the way. Once at the Volga, they would be able to secure the riverbank and drive further north to outflank the defenders. At the same time, 71. and 295. Infanterie-Divisionen, 100. Jäger Division and the Gruppe *Schwerin* battlegroup formation were to make a series of diversionary attacks around the front, in the process providing flanking protection for the main assaults. In the Factory District assault, 305. Infanterie-Division had been allocated Pionier-Bataillone 50, 294 and 336 (plus the staff of Pionier-Bataillon 672), while 389. Infanterie-Division had received Pionier-Bataillone 45 and 162. Here Linden himself clarifies the battle plan:

> After my reconnaissance, I made my proposal to use the pioneers. Because the division had employed its three infantry regiments in the forward line and the division commander placed the attack *Schwerpunkt* [main focus] with the middle regiment, I proposed that each infantry Regiment to be supported by a pioneer battalion in the following order: Pionier-Bataillon 294, Pionier-Bataillon 50, Pionier-Bataillon 336 with 305. Infanterie-Division and Pionier-Bataillone 162 and 389 with 389. Infanterie-Division. I placed Pionier-Bataillon 305 behind Pionier-Bataillon 50 in the sector of the spearhead regiment of 305. Infanterie-Division as a reserve.
>
> The assault would be launched on 11 November 1942. For the time of the attack, I chose the first light of day after the appropriate preparatory fire. Strong pioneer assault groups (at least platoon strength) would push themselves into their starting positions under the protection of the fire, then the artillery would

Vasily Grigoryevich Zaitsev

Arguably the most famous of the front-line riflemen during the battle of Stalingrad was the sniper Vasily Grigoryevich Zaitsev, who during the battle served with the 1047th Rifle Regiment, 284th Rifle Division. Born in Yeleninskoye, Orenburg Governorate, on 23 March 1915, Zaitsev grew up hunting wolves, deer, bear and other prey in the Ural Mountains, developing a real talent with a bolt-action rifle. On the outbreak of war, Zaitsev at first served with the Soviet Navy, as a clerk in Vladivostok, before transferring to the infantry in time for the German assault on Stalingrad. It was in Stalingrad that Zaitsev forged his legendary reputation. He not only killed 243 Germans, but also became responsible for sniper training at the front; it

is estimated that snipers trained by Zaitsev accounted for more than 3,000 Germans. Zaitsev was as much known for his tactical wiliness as his skill with a rifle. In January 1943, however, he was wounded in the eyes by an exploding mortar shell, although he later recovered much of his sight. In February 1943, Zaitsev was awarded Hero of the Soviet Union, and became much lauded in the Soviet press. He later returned to active service in the battle for Germany in 1945, and after the war worked in the textile industry as an engineer and later a factory director. Zaitsev died on 15 December 1991, and although he was initially buried in Kiev he was, in 2006, reburied in the Mamaev Kurgan in what is now Volgograd.

be abruptly advanced; after this, the pioneers will advance in the first wave and penetrate to their objectives while overcoming the enemy in known positions. Once there, they would immediately set themselves up for defence. Infantry would follow as the second wave and clear the enemy from the intermediate ground and subsequently take over the defensive line. (Quoted in Mark 2006: 74–75)

Although the German plan was 'clean' in outline, in reality it was unpredictable and fraught with dangers, and was recognized as such by Linden and other German commanders. The launch of the action was scheduled for 11 November, to give time for all the engineering battalions to gather at the Stalingrad front line. During 9–10 November, however, the Soviets made strong attacks of their own in the Factory District, particularly against 79. Infanterie-Division. All the attacks were deflected, but for a time they complicated the launch of the German action. Yet some German gains were made – on the 9th, Pionier-Bataillone 100 and 295, supported by units from 100. Jäger-Division and 295. Infanterie-Division, made an attack of their own, capturing the important oil refinery in the Mamaev Kurgan sector. The acquisition of this position further strengthened the German offensive capability against the Factory District, and the operation was ready to go.

A German infantry section in a factory. Linden described the landscape: 'The terrain in the gun factory area was a gigantic field of rubble that gently fell away to the Volga – right up to the steep slope of the riverbank. The ruins of the numerous workhalls were still partly standing with their steel frameworks and individual corrugated iron walls … The underground vaults of the workhalls … had been turned into command posts and strongpoints. Iron parts, wreckage of machines, gun barrels of all calibres scattered about in enormous quantities, T-beams, corrugated iron and massive craters made the entire terrain impassable. Panzers could not operate in this terrain. Trenches … served as approach routes to the forward positions because the positions on the forward slope could be seen by the enemy' (quoted in Mark 2006: 74). (Nik Cornish at Stavka)

1 0355hrs: Assault teams from 1./PiBtl 305 and Grenadier-Regiment 578 commence their attack on the L-shaped Apotheke building, capturing it in a superb lightning assault that also takes 45 prisoners. Elements of the force then maintain the momentum, attacking from the Kindergarten building and the Apotheke down into the 'Index-Finger Gulley' by 0930hrs, where they meet up with elements of Pionier-Bataillon 294 on the banks of the Volga.

2 0400hrs: Grenadier-Regiment 576 launches a powerful attack against the boundary between the 241st and 161st Rifle regiments, with Kampfgruppe *Seydel* making a supporting attack against the 161st Rifle Regiment on Grenadier-Regiment 576's right flank. Pionier-Bataillon 294 and 2./PiBtl 305 are at the forefront of the attack, working in small groups and attempting to dislodge the Soviet defenders from stubborn positions. The Soviet riflemen put up a dogged defence, essentially stopping the German onslaught by dawn.

3 0400hrs: Pionier-Bataillon 45 and Grenadier-Regiment 546 begin their push down through the apartment buildings around the Prospekt Lenina against the 344th and 768th Rifle regiments. At terrible cost the German units manage to drive their way through to Finger Gulley, but heavy Soviet fire from the opposite bank means they have to stop and dig in, defending themselves against subsequent counter-attacks.

4 0930hrs: Grenadier-Regiment 576 regroups and makes two more attacks against the 241st Rifle Regiment, launching the attacks at 0930hrs and 1130hrs. The Soviet resistance progressively crumbles under the impact of heavy casualties, and eventually gives way sufficiently for numbers of combat engineers and infantry from Grenadier-Regiment 576 to reach the Volga behind the Fuel Tanks, where they remain under fire from the opposite bank and from Soviet defenders emplaced in the riverbank.

5 c.1030hrs: Soldiers from the 650th Rifle Regiment and the Barrikady workers' militia succeed in halting a major German attack on the Kommissarhaus, launched just before dawn by Grenadier-Regiment 578, with Panzer-Pionier-Bataillon 50 and elements of Sturmkompanie 44 leading the attack. Despite the support of six 15cm sIG 33B self-propelled guns, the German attack is stopped with heavy additions to a lengthening casualty list.

6 1100hrs: Having fought their way down across the Soviet front line with Sturmschwadron 24, troops from Pionier-Bataillon 162 manage to reach the Volga bank at Dorn-Rachel (Thorn Gulley) and swing southwards against the 768th Rifle Regiment and elements of the 118th Guards Rifle Regiment.

7 1400hrs: The 344th and 650th Rifle regiments restore and hold the Soviet line, having mounted a particularly trenchant defence of key buildings around the Prospekt Lenina in the face of a German assault starting at 0400hrs and conducted by Grenadier-Regiment 577, Pionier-Bataillon 336, 3./PiBtl 305 and elements of Sturmkompanie 44.

8 c.1700hrs: By this time Pionier-Bataillon 389, having begun its attack at 0600hrs, has managed to fight through the Soviet resistance in the northerly sector of the attack and has fanned out along the riverbank, consolidating a stretch of 500m along the side of the waterway. Combined with the other elements of the day's advances for the Germans, this achievement traps the defenders in an ever-shrinking pocket along the Volga, although the levels of Soviet resistance remain ferocious.

Battlefield environment

The action of 11 November 1942 was fought in the fine weather that had characterized the month so far, with freezing temperatures but bright sunshine and dry roads and surfaces. The good weather was of scant comfort to the Germans, however, as it also meant that the Soviet defenders had good visibility; the Germans had no cover from adverse weather, although conversely this also aided more rapid offensive movement. The battle itself was now mainly fought in the apartments and administrative buildings below the main factory area. These varied in nature, from low-rise schoolhouses to multi-storey apartments, the latter framing streets in regularly spaced blocks, forming nightmarish kill zones for attackers. The battlefield also included the fortress-like structure of the Kommissarhaus (Commissar's House), set in relatively open ground. The battlefield was ripped and torn by this stage of the fighting, the buildings often featuring collapsed ceilings and floors, barricaded corridors, rubble-clogged stairwells and no internal lighting.

A German MG 34 team takes up a defensive position in the ruins of a collapsed building. Note the way in which the smooth contours of their steel helmets stand out quite clearly against the jagged angles of the rubble. This was one reason why German soldiers had to exercise extreme caution in exposing their heads to Soviet snipers. (Nik Cornish at Stavka)

BARRIKADY FACTORY DISTRICT

LOWER
SETTLEMENT

544

389

162

44

546

45

768

118
Gds

8

6

Dorn-Rachel
(Thorn Gulley)

Landeplatz-Rachel
(Landing Strip Gulley/
Finger Gulley)

577

7

336

3   305

44

50

1   578

1   305

294

2

576

2   305

344

PRIBALTISKAYA

PROSPEKT LENINA

TAIMYRSKAYA

Rote Haus
(Lyudnikov's OP)

Lyudnikov's CP

Park

5

650

241

138

Kommissarhaus

578

Kindergarten

Apotheke

4

576

Fuel tanks

95

XX

Blinddarm-Rachel
(Appendix Gulley)

ARBATOVSKAYA

STALNAYA

TUVINSKAYA

MEZENSKAYA

uppe
eydel

MASHINNAYA

PERENOVSKAYA

TIKHORSKAYA

NOVOSELSKAYA

RAZDOLNAYA

GRANTI

161

Zweifinger-Rachel
(Two-Finger Gulley)

Volga

N

0   200yd

0   200m

INTO COMBAT

The following account of the actions around the Barrikady Gun Factory is of necessity broken down into individual sectors, to aid comprehension. It should be noted, however, that in fact the attacks surged forward largely simultaneously. Combined with the offensive drive across the Stalingrad front, the fighting of 11 November was 6. Armee's determined attempt finally to poleaxe the Soviet defence in the city.

The most southerly of the Factory District attacks was launched by Grenadier-Regiment 576, supported by Pionier-Bataillon 294 and 2./PiBtl 305. Tactically, the combat engineers were arranged into c.20-strong assault detachments; across the front, they did not assault as single-battalion entities, but rather were mixed closely into the infantry units. They not only carried their typical burden of grenades, demolition charges and flamethrowers, but also had ladders, axes, wire- and bolt-cutters, spades and hatchets – utility tools would be essential if the pioneers were to force their way into the barricaded Soviet positions.

Grenadier-Regiment 576's objectives were the fuel installations in the south of the Barrikady sector, aiming the main force of the punch at the boundary between the 241st and 161st Rifle regiments. To the right of Grenadier-Regiment 576, Kampfgruppe *Seydel* would attack the 161th Rifle Regiment, while also providing supporting fire to the surge of Grenadier-Regiment 576. The Soviet riflemen of the 241st Rifle Regiment would require all their defensive skills to oppose the attack, as just 340 of them held the sector, distributed among two battalions.

At 0400hrs across the front, German artillery began pounding the target area, striking just in front of the pioneer and infantry spearheads as they advanced along with three assault guns, which were used to target windows and other apertures with heavy destructive fire. Immediately, the Soviets responded with their customary rippling fire from automatic weapons – the Germans in Stalingrad often scratched their heads in dark wonderment at the seemingly limitless supplies of Soviet ammunition – plus startlingly accurate sniper fire. Several of the combat-engineer assault-team leaders were killed or wounded in short order, and the commander of II./GR 576, Major Wilhelm Braun, was trapped in his command position and so was unable to provide guidance. The combat-engineer force demonstrated considerable drive and bravery, even so. At one point, a small group of c.25 men actually managed to bypass positions of resistance and reach the Volga. There, however, they were isolated and destroyed to a man by the Soviet troops along the banks.

By the time dawn started to light the smoke and brick dust hanging over Stalingrad, the attack by Grenadier-Regiment 576 was effectively stalled. The Soviet defenders had once again shown their utter tenacity. Particularly noteworthy were the efforts of one Fedor Filippovich Manenkov. Armed with a 14.5mm anti-tank rifle (either a single-shot PTRD or the semi-

A Soviet artillery unit emplaced at Stalingrad. Note the substantial cover built up around each gun, in the form of earth banks, which would have provided some protection from inevitable German counterfire or Luftwaffe bombardment. Despite their best efforts, the Germans were never able to suppress the Red Army artillery. (AirSeaLand Photos/Cody Images)

automatic PTRS-41), Manenkov managed to destroy two of the assault guns and severely damaged a third, despite coming under tremendously heavy fire that killed most of the individuals around him. By the time the Barrikady fight was over, Manenkov would be credited with six tank kills, an achievement that led to his being granted the Order of Lenin.

The heavy losses sustained in the initial assault meant that Major Braun had to halt and regroup his forces, and pull in his reserves, before he could launch an attack again. This he was able to do at 0930hrs. This time, the defenders of the 241st Rifle Regiment began to crumble, not through lack of willpower but simply through losses mounting to a critical level. The Germans also made some tactical breakthroughs, particularly in the use of flamethrower assaults to snuff out Soviet defenders in the sewage canal system and building basements. The handful of Soviet riflemen held on with astonishing grit, but a further German attack at 1130hrs managed to puncture the thin shell of defence and combat-engineer and infantry troops now reached the Volga.

On the left flank of Grenadier-Regiment 576 was Grenadier-Regiment 578, which was supported for the offensive by Panzer-Pionier-Bataillon 50, 1./ PiBtl 305 and elements from Sturmkompanie 44. They were faced with two ominous building objectives. First, there was the large L-shaped Apotheke factory, and next to it, across Arbatovskaya Avenue, the Kommissarhaus, so called by the Germans because it had housed NKVD troops. The Kommissarhaus was in fact the main administrative building of the Barrikady, a U-shaped three-storey building built in a castle-like fashion, with 1m-thick walls, wings terminating in keep-like structures and underground tunnel networks. Held by men of the 241st Rifle Regiment, it posed a formidable objective.

Like its southerly neighbour, Grenadier-Regiment 578 began its attack behind the supporting artillery barrage shortly before 0400hrs, launching

A German assault team moves forward from the protection of a gulley. The man at the front is carrying a 7.92mm MG 34 general-purpose machine gun, while the men to the left of the image appear to carry the tripod and ammunition canisters. (AirSeaLand Photos/Cody Images)

off from Haus 53. Combat engineers from 1./PiBtl 305, led by Leutnant Hans Zorn, advanced unobserved up to the walls of the Apotheke, and laid explosive charges intended to blow open entrances (the Soviet troops had barricaded the doors and windows). The charges were detonated at 0355hrs, their heavy blasts ripping new apertures and stunning the defenders. There followed a lightning assault by the combat engineers, backed by the infantry. With an unrelenting tempo and the liberal use of grenades, each floor and room was cleared. Such was the competence and surprise of the attack, that 45 prisoners were taken.

Around 0930hrs, the third and fourth assault teams of Grenadier-Regiment 578 pushed from the Kindergarten building and the Apotheke factory down into the 'Index-Finger Gulley', one of the numerous watery cuts that sliced into the sandy banks of the Volga. They managed to gain control over the gulley, silencing Soviet defence points dug into the banks, then launched an attack on the nearby Haus 79, which was quickly taken, the surprised Soviet defenders overcome. Pionier-Bataillon 294 also pushed up from the south to join Grenadier-Regiment 578 at Index-Finger Gulley.

The Kommissarhaus, in contrast to the Apotheke, proved far more obstinate. Its defenders were a mixed group – part soldiers from the 650th Rifle Regiment, and part men of the Barrikady workers' militia. In the vanguard of this attack were the combat engineers of Panzer-Pionier-Bataillon 50, attacking out from Haus 56, with supporting movement on the opposite flank by elements of Sturmkompanie 44, with Haus 72 as its launch point. The combat engineers had adopted a different timing for their attack when compared with that for the assault on the Apotheke. They waited until first light, the visibility of dawn then allowing them to advance and place wall-breaching charges more accurately. Unfortunately, the light also meant that the Soviet defenders could see their approach, and soon the combat engineers were under the most harrowing fire. The looming U-shape of the Kommissarhaus meant that the angles of small-arms fire and grenade arcs were numerous and overlapping. One Soviet soldier later recorded:

Giving instructions in the centre of the picture here is Oberleutnant Friedrich Winkler, a company commander in II./GR 577 during the November offensives in Stalingrad. Born on 22 August 1909 in Worms, he joined the German Army in the 1930s, signing up to a 12-year period of service. His initial unit was Infanterie-Regiment 56, but in June 1942 he was posted, with the rank of *Oberleutnant*, to 305. Infanterie-Division, specifically to the Stabskompanie/IR 577, which in turn became Grenadier-Regiment 577 in October. Winkler was in the thick of some of the worst fighting in the Stalingrad campaign, being heavily involved as a company commander during the actions in the Factory District during October and November 1942. Following the Soviet encirclement of Stalingrad, Grenadier-Regiment 577 was progressively destroyed, and Winkler fell into Soviet captivity in February 1943. He lasted but a few days of imprisonment, dying at the age of 34 on 8 February 1943 in Kriegsgefangenlager *Beketowka*. (NARA)

On 11 November 1942, the fascists were all fired up to capture the factory administration building. A company of Germans concentrated in shell craters not far from the defences of our building. Their destruction was necessary because they were assembling their attack. For this task, militiaman Fedin grabbed some grenades, left the building and under cover of the submachine-gunner Putirin, tossed grenades at the Germans, forcing the survivors to give up and then take flight. Even though they were now further away, we did not lose our heads. Fedin was wounded in this fighting but stopped advancing forward and carried on fighting. Many of the militia died bravely in defence of the Barrikady factory. (Quoted in Mark 2013: 106)

For the men of Panzer-Pionier-Bataillon 50, casualties reached such a level – 17 men killed and 60 wounded – that they were compelled to retreat. In an attempt to turn the situation around a force of ten assault guns, including six 15cm sIG 33B self-propelled guns, was sent forward to hammer breaches in the defences and provide suppressive fire at close range. Yet the assault guns were unintelligently applied, moving without adequate infantry support into the range of Molotov cocktails, anti-tank grenades and anti-tank-rifle fire. The level of loss is unclear, but it appears certain that at least four of the six sIG 33B assault guns were either knocked out or seriously damaged, many of the crewmembers shot dead as they attempted to flee their vehicles. Thus by mid-morning, the attack against the Kommissarhaus had stalled and would essentially remain so for the rest of the day, fundamentally destabilizing the frontal integrity of the German offensive.

A famous close-up photograph of Oberleutnant Winkler. Note how half of his Infantry Assault Badge has been broken off, probably deliberately. This could be a sign that the wearer might no longer believe in the aims of the war, but was still utterly dependable as a combat soldier. (NARA)

Adjacent to Grenadier-Regiment 578 was Grenadier-Regiment 577, supported by Pionier-Bataillon 336, 3./PiBtl 305 and Sturmkompanie 44. This group's objectives were to move out from positions just below the main factory area, take some of the key buildings bordering Prospekt Lenina, then drive across and through the Lower Settlement to attain the Volga. Principal defenders of these positions were men from the 344th and 650th Rifle regiments, veteran units already heavily bloodied in Stalingrad.

Once the attack began, the experience was grimly familiar. The combat-engineer assault teams attacked the Soviet positions, the initial concentration being on Häuser 66, 67, 73 and 74. The fight for every room and every corridor was unrelenting. For example, soldiers from 2./PiBtl 336 at one point had to make four attempts simply to ascend a staircase from the basement to the next floor of Haus 66, the Soviet riflemen above maintaining a steady barrage of grenades until they were overcome and killed, some of them leaping to their deaths from the roof. It took several hours and many casualties to clear the rest of the house. It should also be remembered that the defenders of the buildings were often few in number. For example, Haus 67 was occupied by just one officer (Lieutenant I.S. Pogrebnyak) and seven men. Yet even such sparse numbers of riflemen gave a good account of themselves, and despite the loss of Haus 66 the Soviet troops largely held out in the sector, while the fighting raged around its flanks. In fact, Pionier-Bataillon 336 was even forced out of its captured building by counter-attacks from the 344th Rifle Regiment, the Soviet assaults restoring and then holding the line by 1400hrs.

The final major strand to the Barrikady offensive on 11 November was the push by 389. Infanterie-Division, well supported by the skills and manpower of Pionier-Bataillone 45, 162 and 389. Attacking from Manufacturing Hall 6a, 2./PiBtl 45 would assault towards Haus 78; 3./PiBtl 45, on its left flank, down the avenue between Haus 78 and the adjacent block of apartment buildings; and 1./PiBtl 45 through the apartment blocks towards Prospekt Lenina. Grenadier-Regiment 546 would be the infantry unit supporting this assault; the defending Soviet units were the 344th (facing 2./PiBtl 45) and 768th Rifle regiments. Nearby, backed by Grenadier-Regiment 546 and Sturmschwadron 24, Pionier-Bataillon 162 would take a straight line of attack down the avenue leading up to the apartment block, pushing across Prospekt Lenina and then fanning out to positions on the Volga bank. Defence in this sector came from the 768th Rifle Regiment and, on the right flank, 1/118th GRR; the 118th Guard Rifle Regiment was part of the 37th Guards Rifle Division. Finally, against 1/118th GRR and 2/118th GRR, Pionier-Bataillon 389 would attack at the very northern edge of the German front line, swinging inwards towards the Pionier-Bataillon 162 assault and again heading for the Volga bank. The overall ambitions of the attack were also to split the 344th Rifle and 118th Guards Rifle regiments, plus capture Lyudnikov's observation post, in a building called the *Rote Haus* (Red House) plus his command post, set further back on the bank of the Volga.

For Pionier-Bataillon 45, the initial experience of the assault (which began at 0330hrs) was appalling, with multiple casualties taken quickly, including from a sniper-supported counter-attack from the Soviet riflemen. One German soldier, Bertold Paulus, noted that in an objective area measuring 500m by 200m there was a Soviet defensive bunker about every 10m, and each had to be destroyed in turn, at close quarters and even through hand-to-hand fighting. Pionier-Bataillon 45 made achingly slow progress, and during its advance down Palets Ovrag (Finger Gulley) it was shelled to a stop by responsive Soviet artillery from across the river, firepower that prevented the command post of the 768th Rifle Regiment's Major Gunyaga falling into German hands. The men of Pionier-Bataillon 45 consolidated their gains, fending off several Soviet counter-attacks.

For Pionier-Bataillon 162, the biggest initial hurdle was the Soviet front-line defences, set around a raised railway embankment. Through focused flanking attacks that probed the boundary between the 118th Guards Rifle Regiment and the 768th Rifle Regiment, plus generally excellent assault coordination, the combat engineers and Sturmschwadron 24 managed both to reach the Volga at Dorn-Rachel (Thorn Gulley) and to surround the beleaguered 118th Guards Rifle Regiment. At 1100hrs, after regrouping, the combat engineers began a hard drive southwards down the Volga bank. A noose was closing around the 768th Rifle Regiment, and small groups of Soviet riflemen were channelled into desperate acts of local defence. The

German troops were forced to pull back and regroup, launching yet another costly attack at 1330hrs. This time Gunyaga's command post was threatened, and in a startling moment Lyudnikov – no less than a division commander – personally went up to see Gunyaga to bolster his resistance, his coat being slashed by grenade fragments along the way.

In the evening of an exceptionally bloody day, Pionier-Bataillon 162 and the other units launched yet another series of repeated attacks. The shattered survivors of the 118th Guards Rifle Regiment were forced to flee or die.

Meanwhile, Pionier-Bataillon 389 had also attacked, although later, at 0600hrs. In a rapid movement, aided by the short distance to the Volga at that point, combat engineers quickly reached the river, in the process cutting off part of 2/118th GRR (Mark 2013: 123). The German force spread out along the shore, facing frequent Soviet resistance from small groups, but eventually secured about 500m of the riverbank, an extraordinary gain in the context of the Stalingrad city battle. Even so, despite the huge investment of energy and blood, the Soviet resistance had still not collapsed. General der Artillerie Walther von Seydlitz-Kurzbach, commander of LI. Armeekorps, summed up the situation accurately at 1715hrs, in a report to 6. Armee:

> The attack of 305. and 389. Infanterie-Divisions have had no decisive success. 305. Infanterie-Division gained the Volga cliffs east of the fuel installation and then advanced to the next gulley north of there. 389. Infanterie-Division won the bank of the Volga along a 500-metre front, joining it up with the previously occupied river bank. The assaults of both divisions were halted in the face of bitter and obstinate enemy resistance ... Objective for 12 November: prepare for the continuation of the attack east of the Gun Factory on 13 November. (Quoted in Mark 2006: 143)

In this dramatic image, four Soviet submachine-gunners (one armed with a captured MP 40) engage attacking Germans from an office room, one soldier twisting under the impact of a bullet. It was generally inadvisable to adopt a firing position directly framed by a window; a position back in the room's shadows was safer. (Photo by Keystone-France/Gamma-Keystone via Getty Images)

The assault around the Kommissarhaus

13 November 1942

BACKGROUND TO BATTLE

The German offensive of 11 November 1942 had not been lacking in fury, death and exceptional bravery, but it had been short on decision. Some German gains had been made around the Barrikady Gun Factory, and a fresh slab of the Volga was under German control, but the Soviets had clung on tenaciously to many key landmarks, and showed no sign of collapse. The combat-engineer troops, meanwhile, had suffered terribly for their slim gains. Out of the attacking force of 1,753 men, a total of 440 had become casualties – roughly one in four of all the participants. It was a damaging attrition rate for these expert soldiers.

Across on the other side, the Soviets were also bleeding heavily. In the 138th Rifle Division, the casualty rate was roughly similar to that of the German forces. Yet other forces had been virtually annihilated. The 241st Rifle Regiment, for example, suffered a 117 per casualty rate, having lost 400 men from a pre-attack strength of 340 (Mark 2013: 145). Furthermore, Lyudnikov remained in an extremely perilous situation, with fewer than 1,000 men on the west bank of the Volga, scattered in pockets large and small. Major-General Nikolai Ivanovich Krylov, the 62nd Army's chief-of-staff, summed up the situation:

> The first attack did not bring any decisive success and remained inconclusive ... Only after committing his reserves was the enemy able to perform a major strike south of the Barricades factory ... splitting our army a third time. The isolated

'island' that formed between the main forces of the army and the Northern Group ran 700 metres along the bank with a depth of 450 metres only. It included the northeastern part of the 'Barricades', several adjacent streets and the slope leading down to the Volga, rugged with ravines. This was Lyudnikov's 138th Division. (Quoted in Joly 2014: 107)

Although this third combat chapter focuses on the clashes of 13 November, in reality there was a continuity of fighting during 11–25 November. During the night of 11/12 November, localized nocturnal battles rippled up and down the lines; the Soviets had already established an unnerving reputation for night fighting among the fatigued German forces at Stalingrad. On the 12th itself, several attacks were made by both sides in an effort to swing the tactical situation back in their favour. The reconstituted 241st Rifle Regiment managed to claw back the Fuel Tanks sector after several repulsed attacks, defending the positions until, at 1400hrs, a major German attack once again reclaimed the fuel tanks, although German efforts to advance beyond were crushed. Soviet units also made attempts to reach Lyudnikov's 'island' by advancing up the bank of the Volga, but these were beaten off. Some reinforcements from across the river, however, did bolster the strength of the Soviet resistance.

In the high command of 6. Armee, it was felt that the Soviets were stunned and staggering from the initial blow, but that it would need a further major

Soviet riflemen worked in close cooperation with artillery units, often building street barricades that would channel German armour into anti-tank kill zones. The gun here is a 76mm divisional gun M1942 (ZiS-3), the most numerous Soviet field-artillery type of the war. (AirSeaLand Photos/Cody Images)

A picture of 'Pavlov's House', and its eponymous defender. The house was an apartment building that overlooked the bank of the Volga, and it held out under 60 days of siege by the Germans from 27 September to 25 November 1942. Sergeant Yakov Pavlov, the commander of the platoon that held the building, himself often fired from the roof against German armour using an anti-tank rifle. (AirSeaLand Photos/ Cody Images)

assault to attain the much-needed victory. LI. Armeekorps was issued with broad next-day objectives at 1645hrs on the 12th, which basically instructed the corps to continue the attack with assault-group methods until the Volga bank east of the Barrikady Gun Factory was secure.

For this renewed onslaught, there would be some reorganization of the combat-engineer units acting in support. Taking account of the losses suffered on 11 November, for the 13 November onslaught just three of the combat-engineer battalions would once again be thrown into the maelstrom as spearhead forces. This was not entirely a matter of choice. At midnight on 12/13 November, the 685th Rifle Regiment launched an attack in the Fuel Tanks sector, and Grenadier-Regiment 576, with Pionier-Bataillon 294, would spend the night and most of the next day in a defensive role, countering the determined Soviet push. The main combat-engineer units dedicated to offensive actions, therefore, were Pionier-Bataillone 50, 162 and 336. The soldiers of Pionier-Bataillone 50 and 162 would be the point men for Grenadier-Regiment 578, along with Sturmkompanie 44. Launching off from Haus 79, already close to the Volga bank, their objective was to push towards and hopefully take the Kommissarhaus, while also extending the depth of their control over the riverside. Grenadier-Regiment 577, meanwhile, supported by Pionier-Bataillon 336, would strike out northeastwards along Pribaltiiskaia Street and Prospekt Lenina, clearing the Soviet forces from the apartment blocks along the routes. These two attacks would, the Germans hoped, also cut out the pocket in which the 138th Rifle Division was still making a valiant stand.

For Linden, the application of 'assault group methods' was causing him no small measure of concern. The ranks of his engineers – elite soldiers with a very specialist range of skills – were being thinned out at an alarming rate, and they could not be replaced easily. Nor was there any sign that the objectives of the 13th would be any easier to achieve than those of the 11th. Even the Volga had been fortified to a degree, the Soviet troops gouging cave-like dug-outs into the banks. It was clear to Linden that if the fighting continued as it had been doing, the pioneers would cease to exist as an effective and substantial force. At least the high command permitted the implementation of some common-sense measures, such as the digging of approach trenches so that soldiers could advance to their laying-up positions relatively free from the threat of snipers and other depredations. (Soviet artillery had inflicted many casualties on the Germans even as they gathered themselves for the 11 November offensive.)

In addition to the fighting, both sides had to contend with the increasing onset of winter. The day itself was clear and bright, with sunshine glaring down on a hard frost. Although there was, as yet, none of the fearsome Russian snowfall, the temperatures were extremely low, dropping down to -15°C during the night-time hours. Such cold made handling weapons, and indeed touching any metal surface, a freezing experience.

A Soviet rifleman clambers over a pile of rubble to his next position, his comrade on the right providing him with covering bursts from his PPSh-41. The soldier in the front centre is wearing the *telogreika* quilted jacket, which was largely superior as cold-weather clothing to anything widely available to the Germans at this time. (AirSeaLand Photos/Cody Images)

1 0345hrs: Pionier-Bataillon 162, in support of Grenadier-Regiment 578, launches the 13 November German attacks with a concerted push out from the Apotheke, advancing to the south of the Kommissarhaus and aiming for Lyudnikov's CP building, while Panzer-Pionier-Bataillon 50 supports the attack further north. Pionier-Bataillon 162 suffers extremely heavy casualties at the hands of the 650th Rifle Regiment, and also from fire coming out from the Kommissarhaus, and they fail to take the CP. At the same time, Grenadier-Regiment 578 drives for the bank of the Volga, but is stopped by a spirited counter-attack from the 179th Separate Engineer Battalion, and other Soviet units in the area.

2 0345hrs: Grenadier-Regiment 577 and Pionier-Bataillon 336 attack the key apartment buildings held by elements of the 344th and 650th Rifle regiments, principally focusing their efforts on taking Häuser 66, 67 and 73. Extremely heavy close-quarters fighting develops in and around the buildings, with the Soviet troops launching small-scale counter-attacks to drive back or halt the Germans.

3 c.1310hrs: Combat engineers of Panzer-Pionier-Bataillon 50, alongside Sturmkompanie 44, launch a new assault on the fortress of the Kommissarhaus. For this attack, they are heavily supported by tanks and assault guns provided by Panzer-Regiment 36 and Sturmgeschütz-Abteilung 254. The German team adopts a new tactic, attempting to move through the main inner courtyard and assault the building via the main entrance.

4 The German assault force moves into the main courtyard of the Kommissarhaus, which is actually less heavily defended than the outer-facing aspect of the building. Keeping close to the inner walls, the Germans advance up to the main entrance.

5 The pioneers use demolition charges to blast their way through the main entrance doors to access the interior.

6 Heavy exchanges of small-arms fire take place on the building's central stairway, as the Soviet defenders attempt to stop the Germans from accessing the second-floor corridors and rooms.

7 The pioneers and troops of Sturmkompanie 44 nevertheless manage to battle their way up to the second floor. They then proceed to clear the building from the upper floor downwards, with separate fighting for the stairs and rooms of the basement areas.

Battlefield environment

The fighting of 13 November was conducted under increasingly wintry conditions, with temperatures remaining well-below zero and a heavy frost hardening the landscape. The salient feature of the day's fighting was the Kommissarhaus. Built in 1915–16, it had a U-shaped layout with bastion-like structures at the end of each wing. The building was powerfully built, with 1m-thick walls and steel-reinforced concrete floors; window apertures were narrow, almost like the arrow slits on a medieval castle, hence the interior was gloomy. The use of the building for administrative purposes meant that the corridors and rooms featured office furniture, books and bookcases, and paperwork, all of which lay about scattered and wrecked. Combat also raged through Soviet housing and apartment blocks, small manufacturing units and along the banks of the Volga. The latter presented a specific tactical challenge, consisting of high, loamy cliffs split through with very deep gullies. The earth held together enough for the Soviet defenders to create dug-outs within the cliff face, some many metres deep.

Soviet troops cautiously ascend a staircase during a clearance operation. Stairways were uniquely dangerous features of contested buildings; the advantage tended to lie with the troops at the top of the stairs, as they had the advantages of gravity on their side when it came to throwing grenades. (Courtesy of the Central Museum of the Armed Forces, Moscow via Stavka)

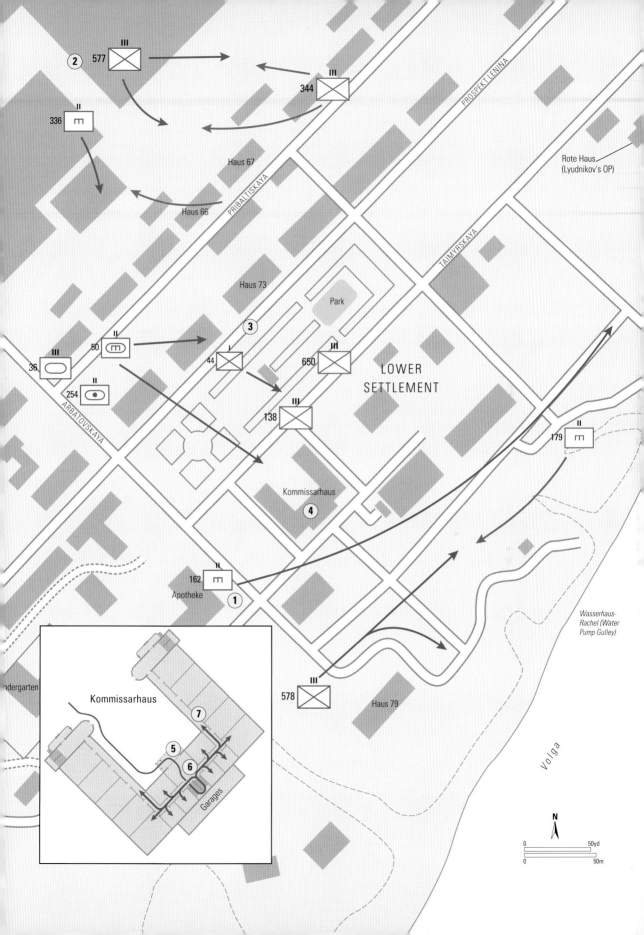

2 577 III

344 III

336 II

Haus 67

PRIBALTISKAYA

Haus 66

PROSPEKT LENINA

Rote Haus
(Lyudnikov's OP)

TAIMYRSKAYA

Haus 73

Park

3

50 II

36 III

44 I

650 III

LOWER
SETTLEMENT

254 II

138 III

179 II

ARBATOVSKAYA

Kommissarhaus

4

162 II

Apotheke

1

Wasserhaus-
Rachel (Water
Pump Gulley)

578 III

Haus 79

Volga

ndergarten

Kommissarhaus

7

5

6

Garages

N

0   50yd

0   50m

INTO COMBAT

The German offensive sprang into life again at 0345hrs on 13 November. At that moment, it was Panzer-Pionier-Bataillon 50 and Pionier-Bataillon 162 which took the lead, attacking with such speed and tempo, and making the most of the cover of darkness, that the Soviet defenders in the area – men of the 650th Rifle Regiment – were largely taken by surprise. Heavy covering fire from machine guns and mortars was laid down from the Apotheke and Haus 79, and the attack also enjoyed the support of 12 tanks and assault guns, this time used with somewhat more tactical caution than on previous occasions.

For Pionier-Bataillon 162, however, the day would not go well. It attempted to attack from beneath the Apotheke towards the Kommissarhaus, and it managed to advance far enough to alarm the Soviet defenders in the Kommissarhaus, as they sensed the threat of encirclement. Furthermore, Lyudnikov's command post was directly challenged. But the Soviets responded with their customary aggression. Senior Lieutenant Ivan Georgiyevich Charashvili, actually a now-gunless artillery officer of the 90th Rifle Regiment, took his surviving battery personnel into action around the Kommissarhaus. He led his team down to the riverbank, personally shooting two German officers on the way, then inflicted heavy casualties on the enemy through showering them with grenades and small-arms fire. Combined with a counter-attack by a mixed force of Soviet riflemen, engineers, security troops and staff

A Red Army machine-gunner, armed with his 7.62mm Degtyaryov DP light machine gun, levels his gun through an improvised firing port. The DP was a solid performer mechanically; its main points of malfunction, however, were the flat pan magazine, which was prone to damage, a rather flimsy bipod and a recoil spring weakened by barrel heat build-up. (From the fonds of the RGAKFD in Krasnogorsk via Stavka)

officers – even Lyudnikov participated – after 10–15 minutes of brutal action the German attack was emphatically quashed, 3./PiBtl 162 being almost entirely destroyed in the action.

Pionier-Bataillon 336 launched its own attack at 0345hrs, driving forward against a series of Soviet building strongpoints, Häuser 66, 67 and 73, held by exhausted elements of the 344th and 650th Rifle regiments. There was hand-to-hand fighting in the darkness. An indication of the localized ferocity of the fighting was that a group of Soviet mortarmen and riflemen managed not only to fight off an assault on their mortar pits by 70 men along Prospekt Lenina, but that the Soviet troops then had the spirit to launch their own small counter-attack, killing ten German soldiers in the process.

One point to note at this stage is that both sides focused on capturing enemy small arms during the actions. Ammunition consumption was so high on both sides that personal weapons were often either running out of ammunition or malfunctioning through overuse. Each side had preferred weapons they liked to capture. For the Soviets, they celebrated when either MG 34s or MG 42s were seized, these GPMGs being superior to the Soviet equivalents. For the Germans, the great prize was the PPSh-41 SMG, known, as noted above, for its perfect match with the requirements of urban warfare. The combat engineers particularly favoured this weapon, often more so than their own MP 40. One key advantage of the Soviet SMG was that its shallow drum magazine allowed the weapon to be fired from the prone position, whereas the lengthy single-stack 32-round box magazine of the MP 40 made such a firing position awkward.

ABOVE LEFT
Few photographs so consummately illustrate the complicated terrain of the Stalingrad battlefield as this one. Soviet troops became adept at using random features such as partially collapsed floors and holes between walls as passageways between positions and strongpoints. (AirSeaLand Photos/Cody Images)

ABOVE RIGHT
A Soviet soldier makes what looks like an ankle-snapping jump from a building during street fighting in Stalingrad. The soldier in the foreground is armed with a Degtyaryov DP light machine gun. Because this was magazine-fed, not belt-fed, it had poor sustained-fire ability, but it was highly battlefield portable. (Photo by Pictorial Parade /Getty Images)

House clearing, 13 November 1942

Men from Pionier-Bataillon 336 and the 334th Rifle Regiment engage in the horrors of house fighting in the apartment buildings along Prospekt Lenina. The Soviet occupiers of the building have piled the stairway full of rubble to prevent easy passage; one German soldier (to the right) is pulling away at a chair in an attempt to clear passage. Bursts of PPSh-41 fire come from the top of the stairs, which the combat engineers are trying to neutralize with a grenade and a return burst of PPSh-41 fire – the Soviet SMG was extremely popular among German troops as well, who often preferred its reliability and magazine capacity to those of the German-issue MP 40. (The distinctive multi-angle muzzle flash of the SMG was caused by the shape of its barrel jacket.) Note the extreme proximity between the German troops and the enemy. Both sides were often in danger of being caught in their own grenade blasts, and fighting with small arms often degenerated into hand-to-hand combat with bayonets and sharpened spades. Even during breaks between the small-unit clashes, the two sides might be within 10–20m of one another, separated only by a corridor or room, or sometimes just a wall. Needless to say, such combat, repeated endlessly, had a psychologically destructive effect on both sides.

Although details about the attack by Pionier-Bataillon 336 specifically are fairly sparse, after-action reports from the 138th Rifle Regiment do illustrate the tenacity of the Germans. Left-flank positions of the division were overrun by 0730hrs, and the division command post came under threat from a group of Germans armed with SMGs. A Soviet counter-attack, however, pushed back the Germans by 1000hrs.

As this action illustrates, despite the pressing of the German attack on 13 November, the Soviets were also in an offensive mind-set, recognizing that they had to keep the Germans under pressure if they were to prevent the enemy from dictating events. The main focus of the Soviet offensive action was around the fuel tanks, under pressure since midnight from Lieutenant-Colonel Evgeny Ivanovich Drogaitsev's 685th Rifle Regiment. One of the biggest Soviet rushes came at about 0850hrs, carried out by a force of *c.*250 men. The assault made solid gains during the initial minutes, bombing and shooting enemy soldiers within their positions and making a 200m advance northwards. Then – as so often during offensive actions at Stalingrad – the Soviet advance failed as attrition took hold. Furthermore, the Germans' intelligent siting of machine guns around the killing zone, emplaced in gullies, trenches and buildings, locked together a lethal crossfire from the front and the flanks so that the Soviets could not push forward any further without virtually certain annihilation.

One of the most critical assaults performed by the combat engineers was their participation in the renewed attempt to capture the Kommissarhaus, delivered by Grenadier-Regiment 578. Despite the relentless pounding the building had received since the battle of Stalingrad began, it was still largely intact structurally. The soldiers inside – principally men of the 138th Rifle Regiment – still diligently guarded this monolithic outpost. By every window, door and corridor angle, the rifleman stacked explosives, grenades, Molotov cocktails, boxes of extra ammunition, hand-to-hand fighting tools – every personal weapon had to be immediately accessible around the clock. The defenders would not give up this building lightly.

Having suffered so dreadfully in their attempt to take the Kommissarhaus two days previously, this time the combat engineers planned the operation far more carefully, and liaised closely with remaining armour units to make the best use of tanks and assault guns, courtesy of Panzer-Regiment 36 and Sturmgeschütz-Abteilung 254. When the German attacks began early in the morning, as before the going was slow towards the building, which bristled with small-arms fire. Yet the German firepower against every visible aperture was relentless, and the occupiers not only had to cope with mounting casualties, but also became preoccupied with fighting fires that whipped up internally, caused by incendiary ammunition and high-explosive shells. At 1310hrs another ten Panzers and assault guns brought their firepower to bear, specifically targeted at the upper floors of the building.

At the appropriate moment, the men of Panzer-Pionier-Bataillon 50 launched their assault against the Kommissarhaus, but this time with a tactical innovation. Instead of attacking around the sides of the building, which were heavily protected by Soviet flanking fire from other buildings, many of the combat engineers instead followed a route inside the 'U' of the Kommissarhaus, moving into the forecourt area by hugging the inner south-east wall. Ironically – and possibly because the Soviets regarded the forecourt as a three-sided killing ground that the Germans would avoid – the inner windows were poorly defended. Thus the combat engineers were able to manoeuvre themselves right up to the central entrance door, which was blown open with demolition charges. The combat engineers were now in the Kommissarhaus, and they would be joined by more of their number using ladders to enter first-floor windows.

This rather posed image of Soviet troops at Stalingrad nevertheless gives a good impression of the types of weapon available to infantry units. From left to right we have a PPSh-41, a PPD-40 (the predecessor of the PPSh-41), a Degtyaryov DP and finally the SVT-38 semi-automatic rifle. (AirSeaLand Photos/ Cody Images)

For the first few minutes, the combat engineers, with extreme caution, moved through the Kommissarhaus uncontested. Their objective was to find a way to the uppermost floor as quickly as possible, and then clear the building from the top downwards, as most of the Soviet defenders were positioned on the lower floors. Once they were on the upper floors, they could attack the Soviets below using shaped charges to blow holes through the floors, through which grenades could be dropped and flamethrowers fired.

Having established machine-gun strongpoints on the ground floor, the combat engineers now began to ascend the staircase to the upper floors. At this point they were detected, and both the Germans and the Soviets fought with the desperation required for survival, as a Soviet account explains:

Hitlerite submachine-gunners managed to break into the stairwell of the central entrance. Combat began inside the building. Mortarmen fought in the right wing of the factory administration building. Soldiers' hand grenades beat off fascist attackers, who made their way along the second-floor corridors ... The Civil Guardsmen and Red Army soldiers held one floor while the fascists controlled the other. There was fighting in each room, each stairwell, each cellar. (Quoted in Mark 2013: 175)

This striking photograph perfectly conveys the extreme caution required for fighting in Stalingrad. These Soviet riflemen, all armed with PPSh-41s, are orienting themselves against a suspected German position. Their actual attack would probably begin with a shower of grenades, bursts of suppressive SMG fire, and a rapid entry into the building. (Courtesy of the Central Museum of the Armed Forces, Moscow via Stavka)

Despite the incredible level of resistance from the Soviet defenders they were, however, unable to prevent the combat engineers from reaching the upper floor. The Soviets were now trapped, and those who were not killed or wounded were forced down into the building's cellars in the early afternoon, the underground space choked with fumes and dust. Once the combat engineers had identified their position, they used their skills in demolitions to finish the job. They unleashed a ghastly explosive assault using satchel charges, ignited petrol cans (to burn up the available oxygen in the cellars and adjacent corridors), and incendiary glass smoke grenades.

The outcome of the fight for the Kommissarhaus was now inevitable. Most of the defenders were killed, and a handful of mentally and physically shattered men surrendered. It was the crowning achievement of the day's operations for the German pioneers. Major Eberhard Rettenmeier, commanding II./ GR 578, described the action thus:

> The assault party of the 50th engineers was re-ordered [reorganized] and equipped with ladders. Simultaneously with the attack on the Commissar's House, an attack was to be launched from House 79 across the open terrain, and the small toehold on the Volga was to be expanded to both sides [the north and south]. Again ... the artillery began the battle with its fire. This time the engineers of the 50th had success. With the aid of ladders, they managed to penetrate into the house through the windows. The Russians fled into the cellars and fortified themselves there. The engineers tore up the floors and closed with the enemy with smoke rounds, explosive ammunition [satchel charges], and petrol. The house was smoking from all apertures, and throughout the day explosions could be heard. Only by evening the Russians disappeared from the cellars and escaped through an exit on the side of the enemy. There was general joy at the command post by evening when the first runner came in from there; by day only radio contact had been possible.
> (Quoted in Glantz & House 2009b: 665)

Taking the Kommissarhaus bought the Germans another large slice of the Factory District and squeezed the Soviet forces even tighter against the riverbank. Yet while Lyudnikov's men were certainly on the back foot, this did not mean that they were beaten. The fighting continued intensively along the Volga bank for the rest of the day and into the night, as other German infantry and combat engineers attempted to extend their control over the Volga and destroy Lyudnikov's 'island' of defence. This was not easy. In the context of the sandy and sloping riverbank, many of the combat engineers' demolitions weapons were ineffective, the explosions often soaked up by the earth or grenades and other devices simply rolling down the riverbank into the water to detonate. Pionier-Bataillon 162 made the best progress in the riverbank actions, securing about 70m of extra terrain, although as usual at grim cost. As night rolled into another day of combat, both sides wondered just what it would take to make the enemy relent.

Analysis

The battle of Stalingrad attracts repeated analysis and reflection within military colleges and thinkers even today, more than 70 years after it was fought. It was by far the most intense, prolonged and costly city engagement of World War II, and as such provided a chaotic laboratory for street fighting and urban warfare tactics. Among learned papers and books on the subject, the battle is often referred to as the 'Stalingrad Academy of Street Fighting'.

LESSONS LEARNT: THE GERMANS

For the German combat engineers, Stalingrad was a place in which their skills were entirely relevant, and hence for the October and November offensives they found themselves at the forefront of the action. One of the greatest lessons for the combat engineers, however, was that they could not operate alone. Indeed, a general lesson of Stalingrad for both sides was that at a tactical level, commanders had to stop thinking in terms of whole-unit movements. The terrain in Stalingrad largely prevented such broad strokes of the pen, as each building, bunker, wrecked factory or house, trench, steel beam, gulley, etc. fractured large units into smaller tactical entities. Hence the combat engineers found themselves frequently divided up into *c.*20-man assault teams, acting with a high degree of localized independence in relation to the objectives in front of them. Yet at the same time, the combat engineers leaned upon the supporting infantry forces, which were often integrated directly into the assault manoeuvre, or acted as immediate follow-up forces to consolidate positions overrun by the combat engineers, or take those positions that had been bypassed.

It was critical during the assault to achieve fire superiority, if possible. This was difficult, not necessarily in terms of generating the right volume of fire (although ammunition consumption and supply did become a problem in many engagements), but regarding targeting. The ruined urban zone provided the Soviets with a near-endless selection of defensive positions, so to be effective the German support fire – from machine guns, mortars, artillery and armour – had to work systematically across the points of resistance, suppressing them in close coordination with the advances of small units of combat engineers and infantry.

Those advancing soldiers also had to read the terrain extremely well if they were to hope for survival. The pervasive presence of Soviet snipers, and the sheer volume of Soviet automatic-weapons fire, meant that exposure on open ground for more than a few seconds typically meant death or serious injury. Thus every feature providing cover or safe approach had to be utilized, even in what might be considered 'rear' areas, as the prolific Soviet artillery had a long reach across the city.

One of the hardest tactical elements for the combat engineers to achieve was *tempo* – the ability to maintain the pace of operations at a level that exceeded the enemy's capacity to resist. Each Soviet position was usually defended with truly astonishing levels of determination. An assault team might spend a costly hour taking a single defended pile of rubble, only to discover the bodies of just two or three men behind it. Actions accessing buildings, and inside buildings, were also costly in terms of manpower and time. Every point of movement – whether window, doorway, coal chute, stairs or corridor – was typically barricaded, and consequently the combat engineers often had to invest time and munitions clearing the obstacles before they could proceed.

The future ahead of the Axis forces captured at Stalingrad was appalling – starvation, mistreatment, disease and forced labour reduced their numbers from 91,000 to fewer than 6,000 survivors released in the 1950s. Here, in 1947, German prisoners are marched back into the city to rebuild it, with the shattered remnants of the Red October Factory in the background. (Photo by Thomas D. Mcavoy/ The LIFE Picture Collection/ Getty Images)

In such close-quarters battle, many of the lessons learned by the combat engineers related to the correct and sequential application of demolitions and firepower. Grenades, stored in plentiful quantities in canvas bags or assault packs, provided them with essentially their own form of throwing-range artillery, ideal for room clearance or for suppressing the enemy for assault. Long hooks were used to scrape away barricades from staircases and doorways while remaining under cover, crowbars found applications in levering up floorboards, while ladders provided the means to access first-floor windows. Demolition charges provided more potent explosive punch than grenades, hence were ideal for blasting out defenders from larger sections of a building or position. As corridors and windows were often hotly contested, the Germans learned to used demolition packs or shaped charges to blow new points of ingress and egress in walls and floors, or to provide firing apertures for SMGs and flamethrowers, as in the final Kommissarhaus assault.

So, most of the 'positive' (always a relative word in Stalingrad) lessons learned by Germany's combat engineers at Stalingrad were refinements of small-unit tactical street-fighting tactics. The negative lessons, however, were fundamental. Every single minor action cost lives and limbs, so regardless of the tactical aplomb demonstrated by the combat engineers, their limited numbers could not cope with the steady grind of attrition. Experience became valued above everything else, as Soviet staff officer Major-General Nikolai A. Talensky noted:

> But during the first stage [of the battle] our losses were, of course, very heavy indeed. And yet, the people who survived acquired a tremendous experience in the technique of house-to-house fighting. Two or three men of such experience could be worth a whole platoon. They knew every drain pipe, every manhole, every shell-hole and crater in and around their particular building, they knew every brick that could serve as shelter. Among piles of rubble, which no tank could penetrate, a man would sit there, inside his manhole or crater, or hole in the floor, and, looking through his simple periscope, he would turn on his tommy-gun the moment he saw any German within firing distance. Seldom anything short of a direct hit could knock him out; he was very hard to pick out of his hole and bombing, as I said before, only tended to create new shelters. (Quoted in Flower & Reeves 1997: 475)

Noting the point made previously about tempo, the combat engineers, and indeed all the German forces in Stalingrad, were faced with a situation light years away from the *Blitzkrieg* vision – a battle they simply couldn't finish, enduring attrition they simply couldn't sustain.

LESSONS LEARNT: THE SOVIETS

It was not only the Germans who learned some critical truths about street fighting. Indeed, if anything, Stalingrad was more formative for the Soviets than for the Germans, as it provided instructive lessons in both urban warfare and defensive fighting – two tactical contexts that had been heavily neglected by the offensively minded high command during the first 18 months of the German–Soviet War.

In the urban fighting, the rifleman and his other infantry associates were central to the outcome of the whole battle. (In a slight qualification to this statement, it must also be recognized that Soviet artillery was also a truly deciding factor, inflicting a round-the-clock attrition upon German forces.) In terms of defence, and as already touched on previously, the rifle regiments learned the value of defence in depth, created by establishing multiple points of resistance with interlocking fields of fire and plenty of firepower. Sometimes these strongpoints were interconnected via trenches, sewerage systems, knocked-through cellars or other means, enabling the covered movement of men between them. But the riflemen also made use of individual strongpoints – typically individual buildings – that became isolated by the Germans but continued to fight on, acting as a kind of tactical sea-anchor, dragging the German forces back as they sought to advance.

Small-unit logistical lessons were also learned by the Soviet riflemen during the battle of Stalingrad, particularly in terms of ammunition supply. Although there remained plenty of issues with ensuring every unit received appropriate volumes of ammunition, by November 1942 the Soviets were largely overcoming the acute lack of weapons and cartridges that existed in the initial months of the battle. The essential importance of ammunition to both the individual soldier and the outcome of the battle is evident in this quotation from Chuikov himself:

> We needed a lot of ammunition, the more the better in fact, because knowing the enemy's intention to wipe out all the troops defending the city as rapidly as possible, we could not, and had no right to, tell the men to use ammunition

The Soviet troops here are wearing the white hooded oversuits that were seen in Stalingrad once the winter snows set in. These oversuits, which provided a good degree of camouflage, were typically worn over the quilted winter uniform. (AirSeaLand Photos/ Cody Images)

sparingly in battle. Our soldiers made sure they always had a proper store of grenades, mortar bombs, bullets and shells. They always said quite openly that they were prepared to tolerate hunger and cold, as long as they were not left without ammunition ... The particular features of fighting in the city made it essential for infantry units to have ample automatic weapons, grenades, and bottles of incendiary liquid. (Chuikov 1963: 207–08, 286)

As noted earlier, the Soviets also innovated in Stalingrad in their offensive tactics, particularly in the ad hoc creation of aggressive 'storm groups'. The emergencies of October and November 1942 reinforced the requirement for what has been termed an 'active defence'. Although many of the minor Soviet attacks described above had little hope of clawing back major portions of territory, what they did achieve was to raise the localized inertia placed upon the German offensive actions, as well as protecting key points such as observation posts and command posts. In addition, it must be acknowledged that integration between the rifleman and artillery assets was increasingly refined in Stalingrad, using every conceivable calibre of artillery piece in both direct- and indirect-fire roles.

The lessons of Stalingrad were of great interest to the Western Allied forces, which in 1942–43 had yet to cut their own teeth in a great city battle. One US report, issued in June 1943 and entitled 'Tactics of Street Fighting on the Russian Front', provides a useful final analysis to the Stalingrad battle, its judgements solid as to why the Germans ultimately failed to claim the city through aggressive attacks:

> These assaults failed to make much progress, partly due to the great quantity of artillery concentrated by the Russians, and partly due to the way in which the large number of reinforced concrete and stone buildings were adapted by the Russians for defense, even when they were in a ruined condition. The Germans were virtually forced to give up large-scale tank attacks as being too costly, and the fighting reverted to intense street fighting between relatively small infantry and engineer assault groups, liberally supplied with flamethrowers. The main difference between the fighting in Stalingrad and that which took place at other inhabited localities along the Eastern Front was that considerable quantities of artillery of every caliber participated on both sides. Many of the Russian batteries were emplaced on the islands and the east bank of the Volga, while others remained among the ruins of the town. The whole site of the city became a complicated tangle of trenches, deep dugouts under blasted buildings, and strongholds in ruins or in the remains of large and strong reinforced concrete buildings, such as abounded in the vast factory area. Here, the theory that the ruins of a city constitute one of the most formidable types of fortification in modern war, was proved to the hilt. (US War Department 1943)

The last two sentences of this passage are especially pertinent to our analysis here. What Stalingrad proved was that urban warfare was a uniquely specialized form of combat, one in which individual and small-unit combat skills, rather than broad tactical movements by larger units, were the deciding factors. The experience of Stalingrad also underlined, particularly for the German forces, why city battles had largely been avoided in the past.

Aftermath

The German offensive launched on 11 November 1942 in Stalingrad marked, by the time it had played itself out, the high watermark of German ambitions on the Eastern Front, and the low point for the Soviet forces. While the combat chapters in this study take the action up to the end of 13 November, the German onslaught continued unabated for more than a week before finally running out of steam by the 25th, although the fighting in Stalingrad would rage on with scarcely diminished intensity for a further two months. By late November, nevertheless, the Soviet grip on the west bank of the Volga had indeed weakened and shrunk, the 62nd Army holding just slivers of territory, bisected by the German advance in the sector between the Tractor Factory and the Red October Factory. And yet, as always, the Soviet forces held on with an almost superhuman resilience. Hitler's ambition finally to sweep the Soviets

Generalfeldmarschall Paulus (left) surrenders at Stalingrad. The day before his surrender, Hitler promoted him to the rank of *Generalfeldmarschall*, doubtless with the expectation that Paulus would commit suicide rather than surrender – no German *Generalfeldmarschall* had ever surrendered. To Paulus's left is the 6. Armee Chief of Staff, Generalleutnant Arthur Schmidt. (AirSeaLand Photos/ Cody Images)

from the west bank of the Volga had failed, and the losses to his already weakened army were profound.

Within the combat-engineer battalions, by the end of December there was scarcely a single soldier left from original battalion complements. Companies might number little more than a few dozen men. It should also be noted that by late November the Russian winter had descended in earnest over the city of Stalingrad, locking the rubble and bodies, alive and dead, under merciless ice and snow. Over the winter months, the temperatures in the city would frequently drop to -30°C and below, adding frostbite and hypothermia to the causes of casualties.

On 19 November an event occurred that completely changed the tactical landscape for 6. Armee in Stalingrad, and indeed the strategic future for the Germans on the Eastern Front as a whole. On that day, at 0730hrs, the Soviet South-West Front and Don Front launched a massive offensive across a 130km front to the north-west of Stalingrad, swinging south and south-east and bulldozing through the Romanian Third Army that essentially formed 6. Armee's northern flank protection. The next day, the Stalingrad Front launched its attack south of Stalingrad city, punching to the west and the north-west and similarly overrunning the Romanian Fourth Army. Even a cursory glimpse at the map revealed the Soviet intentions – Stalin was aiming to encircle the Germans in Stalingrad. This it achieved on 23 November, when the two Soviet drives finally met with one another around Kalach and Sovetsky directly west of the city. Now, trapped inside Stalingrad city, were 6. Armee and part of 4. Panzerarmee – more than a quarter of a million men. Aerial resupply operations, despite the grandiose promises of the head of the Luftwaffe, Reichsmarschall Hermann Göring, were never adequate. A relief operation in December by Generalfeldmarschall Erich von Manstein, utilizing the non-encircled elements of 4. Panzerarmee, failed to break through the tightening Soviet gap. All that remained for the trapped German soldiers now was either to die or to surrender.

Showing just as much dogged endurance in defence as the Soviets had demonstrated previously, the now-starving, frozen and battle-scarred German forces held on throughout January, but in a shrinking pocket of terrain. The Soviets, now replenished and reinforced, launched a massive offensive within the city (Operation *Koltso*) on 10 January, which by the end of the month had taken all the key German-held airfields in Stalingrad (thus depriving the Germans both of aerial evacuation and aerial resupply) and had split the German forces into isolated northern and southern pockets. The inevitable could not be postponed for ever. On 31 January 1943 most of the survivors of 6. Armee, including its commander, Generalfeldmarschall Paulus, surrendered, with XI. Armeekorps – which briefly continued its resistance in defiance of the surrender – doing likewise on 2 February.

Some pockets of Germans, looking to die rather than surrender, fought on in a desperate form of guerrilla warfare for roughly another month, but they were contained and destroyed. The condition of the remaining Germans by February 1943 was graphically described by British war correspondent Alexander Werth, during a visit to the city:

And then, suddenly, at the far end of the yard I caught sight of a human figure.
He had been crouching over another cesspool, and now, noticing us, he was hastily

pulling up his pants, and then he slunk away into the door of the basement. But as he passed, I caught a glimpse of the wretch's face – with its mixture of suffering and idiot-like incomprehension. For a moment, I wished that the whole of Germany were there to see it. The man was probably already dying. In that basement [...] there were still two hundred Germans – dying of hunger and frostbite. 'We haven't had time to deal with them yet,' one of the Russians said. 'They'll be taken away tomorrow, I suppose.' And, at the far end of the yard, besides the other cesspool, behind a low stone wall, the yellow corpses of skinny Germans were piled up – men who had died in that basement – about a dozen wax-like dummies. We did not go into the basement itself – what was the use? There was nothing we could do for them. (Werth 1946: 562)

A celebratory Red Army infantryman waves a communist flag to signify victory at Stalingrad. The Soviet triumph in the battle at Stalingrad gave the Red Army a new-found confidence in its tactical abilities and also fostered a belief that the Germans could be defeated after all. (Photo by Hulton Archive/Getty Images)

It is hard to overstate the impact of the outcome at Stalingrad on both sides. The Soviets were rejuvenated, having proved the ultimate vulnerability of the Wehrmacht. The Germans were conversely stunned, understanding perhaps for the first time that defeat could be an outcome of the conflict. Yet Stalingrad had left an indelible mark on the Red Army and Soviet memory. The Soviets had taken more than a million casualties, the brunt of the losses borne by the humble riflemen. On the other side, the German combat engineers who survived – and they were few – took their place among the tens of thousands who went into Soviet POW camps. Of all those men, only about 5,000–6,000 returned alive in the 1950s. The Wehrmacht and the combat engineers had paid a shocking price for Hitler's insistence that Stalingrad be taken.

UNIT ORGANIZATIONS

German *Pionier-Bataillon*

A German *Pionier-Bataillon* included a battalion headquarters plus three companies, a model that applied to both the *Panzer-Pionier Bataillon* and standard motorized and horse-drawn *Pionier-Bataillone*. The battalion headquarters, numbering about 76 men, would consist of four main elements: headquarters section, signals detachment, combat train and baggage train. It was the three companies, however, that made up the bulk of the roughly 840 men who comprised the battalion. Directing each company was a company headquarters, which was formed from a headquarters section, a signal detachment, combat trains, a maintenance section (for maintaining vehicles and equipment) and also ration and baggage trains. Each of these elements was led by NCOs. The rest of the company was made up from three combat-engineer platoons, each led by a *Leutnant* or another relatively junior officer. The platoons were, in turn, composed of a platoon headquarters unit, which included six motorcycle-riding messenger personnel. Within each platoon, there were three sections of combat engineers, each section consisting of about 15 men. The section leader would typically be armed with an SMG, while support fire would be provided by one combat engineer armed with an MG 34 (later an MG 42), plus three men acting in support of the machine-gunner.

In a motorized battalion, each company (and the HQs, platoons and sections within each company) would be allocated a number of support vehicles: motorcycles (including with sidecars), light and medium cars, and light and medium trucks. In a *Panzer-Pionier Bataillon*, the vehicle allocation would also include light armoured vehicles, particularly half-tracks. Note that a *Pionier-Bataillon* would also be supported by a light engineering supply column.

Soviet rifle regiment

For the Soviet rifle regiments, the tables of organization and equipment (TO&Es) that governed their composition at Stalingrad (at least up to December 1942) were set in July 1942, these reflecting the depletion in manpower suffered during the first year of war. There were three infantry regiments in each division, and each regiment totalled some 1,667 men. Each regiment had its own headquarters section, but also a variety of specialist platoons (mounted reconnaissance, infantry reconnaissance, signal, anti-aircraft machine gun, chemical, pioneer, anti-tank mortar), companies (SMG, anti-tank rifle, medical, supply) and batteries (infantry gun, mortar). At the heart of the regiment, however, were its three infantry battalions. Each battalion had a small battalion headquarters and three rifle companies, each company having an authorized strength of 145 personnel. Within those 145 men, 12 were allocated SMGs and 12 LMGs. In reality at Stalingrad, not only was the company often far below this ideal strength, but also the proportion of SMG-armed men could be higher, particularly in the later months of the fighting. Fire support within the battalion came from a machine-gun company, armed with nine medium machine guns, plus an anti-tank rifle platoon and a mortar company. Further specialist internal battalion support included a medical platoon, a signals platoon and a trains platoon.

It always needs to be recognized that at Stalingrad official TO&Es carried little weight at times, as units and formations were constantly in a state of emergency reorganization, responding to dreadful and continual losses, tactical crises and the need to merge units into ad hoc assault units.

The German ambition for Stalingrad terminated in absolute disaster, as suggested by these abandoned German positions at the end of the fighting. One interesting technical feature about this photograph is the presence of Czech 7.92mm ZB vz.26 light machine guns, known in German service as the MG 26(t). (AirSeaLand Photos/Cody Images)

BIBLIOGRAPHY

Although there are countless books on Stalingrad, many of them give sweeping portraits of the battle rather than very detailed unit and tactical portraits. This is especially true when it comes to the study of German combat engineers during the engagement. The research for this book is therefore indebted to some of the notable exceptions to this rule, particularly the superb and exhaustive works produced by Jason D. Mark and David M. Glantz (with Jonathan House). The titles by these authors listed below are required reading for anyone wanting a truly detailed insight into both German and Soviet combat operations during this epic battle.

Antill, Peter (2007). *Stalingrad 1942*. Campaign 184. Oxford: Osprey.

Axwell, Albert (1997). *Stalin's War Through the Eyes of his Commanders*. London: Arms & Armour Press.

Beevor, Antony (1999). *Stalingrad*. London: Penguin.

Bull, Stephen (2004). *World War II Infantry Tactics: Squad and Platoon*. Elite 105. Oxford: Osprey.

Bull, Stephen (2008). *World War II Street-Fighting Tactics*. Elite 168. Oxford: Osprey.

Chuikov, V.I. (1963). *The Beginning of the Road: The Story of the Battle for Stalingrad*. London: Macgibbon & Kee.

Flower, Desmond & Reeves, James, eds (1997). *The War 1939–1945: A Documentary History*. Boston, MA: Da Capo Press.

Glantz, David M. with House, Jonathan M. (2009a). *To the Gates of Stalingrad: Soviet German Combat Operations April–August 1942 (The Stalingrad Trilogy, Volume 1)*. Lawrence, KS: University Press of Kansas.

Glantz, David M. with House, Jonathan M. (2009b). *Armageddon in Stalingrad: September–November 1942 (The Stalingrad Trilogy, Volume 2)*. Lawrence, KS: University Press of Kansas.

Glantz, David M. with House, Jonathan M. (2014). *Endgame at Stalingrad: December 1942–February 1943 (The Stalingrad Trilogy, Volume 3)*. Lawrence, KS: University Press of Kansas.

Joly, Anton (2013). *Stalingrad Battle Atlas, Volume I, Sep. 13–Oct. 13 1942*. Paris: Staldata Publications.

Joly, Anton (2014). *Stalingrad Battle Atlas, Volume II, Oct. 14–Nov. 18 1942*. Paris: Staldata Publications.

Joly, Anton (2015). *Stalingrad Battle Atlas, Volume III, Nov. 19–Nov. 30 1942*. Paris: Staldata Publications.

Jones, Michael K. (2014). *Stalingrad: How the Red Army Triumphed*. Barnsley: Pen & Sword.

Lucas, James (2000). *German Army Handbook 1939–1945*. Stroud: Sutton.

Mark, Jason D. (2003). *Death of the Leaping Horseman: The 24th Panzer Division in Stalingrad: 12th August–20th November 1942*. Mechanicsburg, PA: Stackpole.

Mark, Jason D. (2006). *Island of Fire: The Battle for the Barrikady Gun Factory in Stalingrad: November 1942–February 1943*. Sydney: Leaping Horseman.

Mark, Jason D. (2013). *Into Oblivion: Kharkov to Stalingrad: The Story of Pionier-Bataillon 305*. Sydney: Leaping Horseman.

McLean, Colonel French L. (2013a). *Stalingrad: The Death of the German Sixth Army on the Volga, 1942–1943: Volume 1, The Bloody Fall*. Atglen, PA: Schiffer.

McLean, Colonel French L. (2013b). *Stalingrad: The Death of the German Sixth Army on the Volga, 1942–1943: Volume 2, The Brutal Winter*. Atglen, PA: Schiffer.

Rottman, Gordon L. (2005). *Soviet Rifleman 1941–45*. Warrior 123. Oxford: Osprey.

Rottman, Gordon L. (2007). *World War II Infantry Anti-Tank Tactics*. Elite 124. Oxford: Osprey.

Rottman, Gordon L. (2010). *German Pionier 1939–45: Combat Engineer of the Wehrmacht*. Warrior 146. Oxford: Osprey.

Thomas, Nigel (2010). *World War II Soviet Armed Forces (1): 1939–41*. Men-at-Arms 464. Oxford: Osprey.

Thomas, Nigel (2011). *World War II Soviet Armed Forces (2): 1942–43*. Men-at-Arms 468. Oxford: Osprey.

US War Department (31 December 1942). 'Training of Russian Automatic Riflemen' in *Tactical and Technical Trends*, No. 15. Washington, DC: US War Department.

US War Department (3 June 1943). 'Tactics of Street Fighting on the Russian Front' in *Tactical and Technical Trends*, No. 26. Washington, DC: US War Department.

Werth, Alexander (1946). *The Year of Stalingrad*. London: Hamilton.

Zaloga, Steven J. & Ness, Leland S. (2009). *Companion to the Red Army 1939–45*. Stroud: The History Press.

INDEX

References to illustrations are shown in **bold**.